NEAB Syllabus Sup

CW01612559

KINETICS AND ORGANIC CHEMISTRY

Graham Curtis

CH03

This booklet is designed to support the syllabus. It contains some material which has been added in order to clarify the syllabus.

The examination will be limited to material specified in the syllabus.

Collins Educational
77–85 Fulham Palace Road
London W6 8JB
An imprint of HarperCollins *Publishers*

Northern Examinations and Assessment Board
Devas Street
Manchester
M15 6EX

first published 1995

Front cover designed by Derek Lee
Printed and bound by Progressive Print (UK) Limited, Leigh-on-Sea, Essex

CH03 Kinetics and Organic Chemistry

3.1 KINETICS

3.1.1 Collision theory

When two substances react, particles (molecules, atoms, or ions) of one substance must collide with particles of the other. However, not all collisions result in a reaction, i.e. not all collisions are productive. This is because particles will only react if they have sufficient energy. This minimum energy for reaction is known as *activation energy* (see also 3.1.3).

For more complicated molecules the orientation of collision is also important, i.e. nucleophilic substitution in a haloalkane will only occur if the nucleophile collides on the opposite side of the molecule from the leaving halogen, (see also 3.2.6).

3.1.2 Maxwell-Boltzmann distribution

In a sample of gas or liquid the molecules are in constant motion and collide both with each other and the walls of their container. Such collisions are *elastic*, i.e. no energy is lost during the collision, but energy may be transferred from one molecule to another. This means that, at a given temperature, molecules in a sample will have a spread of energies about a most probable energy. J. Maxwell and L. Boltzmann drew curves showing how these energies were distributed and a plot of the number of molecules with a particular energy against that energy has become known as a Maxwell-Boltzmann distribution curve (Fig. 3.1).

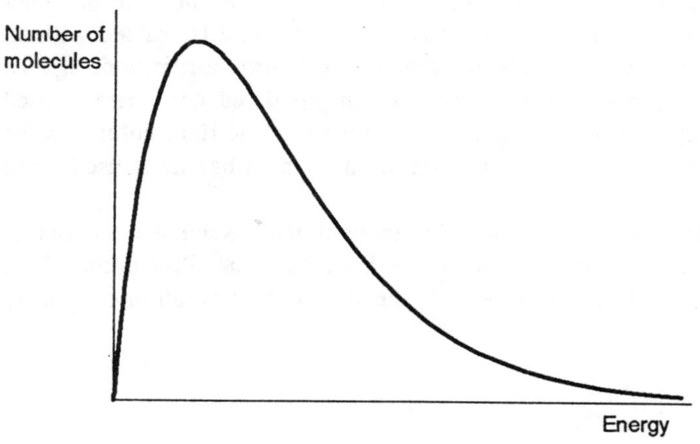

Fig. 3.1 Distribution of energies at one temperature.

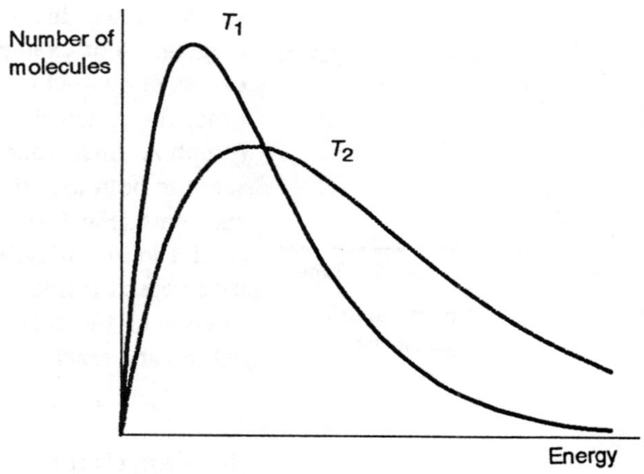

Fig. 3.2 Distribution of energies at two temperatures.

The distribution curve shows that there are no molecules with zero energy and also only a few with very high energies. There is also no maximum energy, the curve approaches zero asymptotically at high energy. The maximum in the curve indicates the most probable energy of a molecule.

Temperature variation

If the temperature of the sample is increased from T_1 to T_2, the average energy of the molecules increases, i.e. the most probable energy of the molecules increases. The spread of energies also increases and the shape of the distribution curve changes as shown in Fig. 3.2. For a fixed sample of gas the total number of molecules in unchanged so the area under the curve remains constant, (see also 3.1.3).

The curve for the higher temperature, T_2, is broader, has a lower peak and, apart from the origin, is always to the right of the lower temperature curve, T_1. The area under both curves, however, is the same as this gives the total number of molecules in the sample.

3.1.3 Factors affecting reaction rate

The rate of a reaction can be defined as the change in amount or concentration of a substance in unit time and has units such as mol dm^{-3} s^{-1}.

If a graph is plotted of the concentration of a reagent or product against time, the rate of reaction at a particular time is given by the gradient of the graph at that time.

The rate is affected by

- the concentration of reagents in solution or the pressure of gaseous reagents
- the surface area of any solid reagent
- the temperature
- catalysts

The collision theory can be used to explain how these factors affect the rate of reaction.

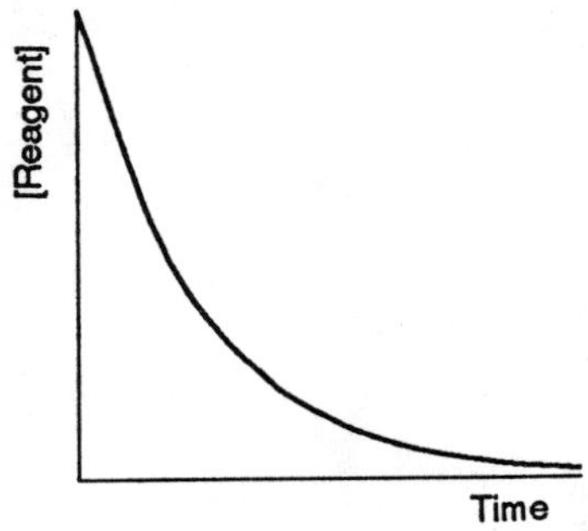

Fig. 3.3 Fall in concentration of reagent with time.

(a) (i) Concentration

Increasing the concentration of a reagent increases the number of particles in a given volume so increases the chance of productive collisions. This will increase the rate of reaction (as long as the reagent appears in the rate equation - see 3.1.4).

As a reaction proceeds, the reagents are being used up so their concentration falls. The rate is therefore at a maximum at the start of a reaction. On a concentration-time graph, the initial gradient is the greatest and the gradient falls to zero at the completion of the reaction (Fig. 3.3).

(ii) Surface area

When one reagent is a solid, the rate of its reaction with a gas or with a substance in solution is increased if the solid is broken into smaller pieces. This increases the surface area of the solid and allows more collisions to occur with particles of the other reagent. For example; when a given mass of calcium carbonate is reacted with an excess of hydrochloric acid and the volume of carbon dioxide produced plotted against time, the gradient of the graph is much steeper when powdered carbonate is used (graph A) than when lumps are reacted (graph B). Note that the final volume is the same in both experiments since the same amount of calcium carbonate is used up in each case (Fig 3.4).

If a solid is dissolved in a solvent, the particles are completely separated so the rate is increased further and the reaction may be almost instantaneous. Precipitates form as soon as the correct solutions are mixed since the free ions in solution can easily collide and react.

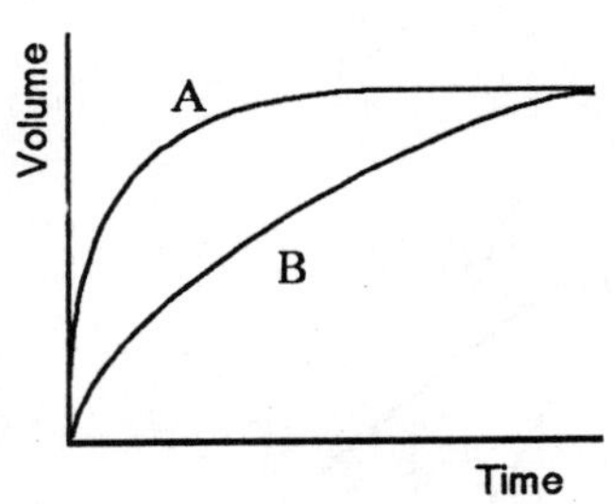

Fig. 3.4 Volume of CO_2 against time

(b) Temperature

An increase in temperature always increases the rate of a reaction. According to the kinetic theory, (see 1.3.4), the kinetic energy of the particles is proportional to the temperature. Particles will have more energy at higher temperatures so they will move about more quickly and there will be more collisions.

More important, however, is that the particles will only react if, on collision, they have more than a minimum amount of energy known as the ***activation energy***.

The activation energy of a reaction is the minimum energy required for the reaction to occur.

At higher temperatures the mean energy of the particles is increased. The Maxwell-Boltzmann curves in Fig. 3.2 show that, if the activation energy for a reaction is E_a, the number of molecules with energy greater than E_a is much greater at temperature T_2 than at the lower temperature T_1. The number of collisions between molecules with sufficient energy to react, i.e. the number of productive collisions, and therefore the rate of reaction will be greater at the higher temperature. Small temperature increases can lead to large increases in rate (see Fig. 3.5).

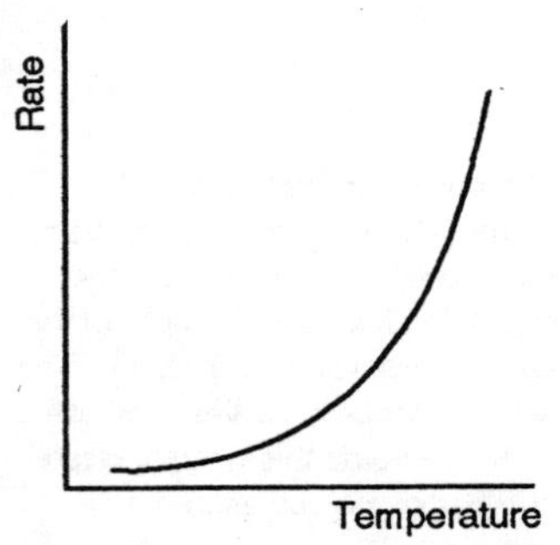

Fig. 3.5 Change of rate as temperature rises

Whether or not a reaction occurs is determined by the energy changes involved, ΔH or more accurately, ΔG (see 4.1.2). However, many reactions with very large negative enthalpies of reaction (or free energy changes of reaction) do not occur spontaneously because the activation energy required is high; e.g.

(i) Petrol reacts with oxygen in air in a very exothermic reaction. But a petrol-air mixture exists in the petrol tank of a car and will only react if sparked.

(ii) The enthalpy change for the conversion of graphite into diamond is only +2 kJ mol^{-1}. The activation energy needed, however, is so high that temperatures of 2000 °C and pressures of 10^7 kPa (10^5 atmospheres) are used in the production of industrial diamonds.

(c) Catalysts

A catalyst is a substance which alters the rate of a reaction without itself being used up. Most catalysts used are positive catalysts, i.e. they increase the rate of reaction. An example of a negative catalyst, i.e. one which slows down a reaction, is lead tetraethyl as used in leaded petrol.

The catalyst operates by providing an alternative mechanism or reaction route of lower activation energy. Fig. 3.6 shows a reaction profile for a catalysed and an uncatalysed reaction. Note that the catalyst has no effect on the overall enthalpy change for the reaction. The catalyst also has no effect on an equilibrium position as it reduces the activation energy of both the forward and the backward reactions.

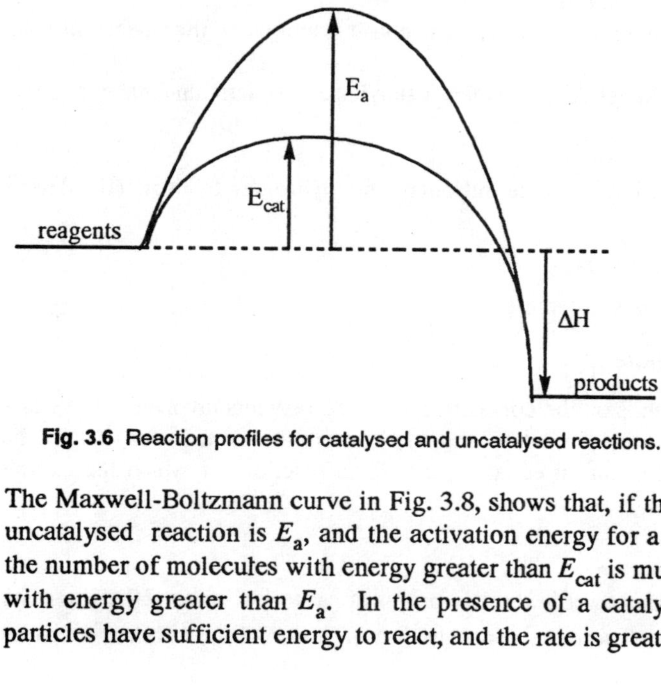

Fig. 3.6 Reaction profiles for catalysed and uncatalysed reactions.

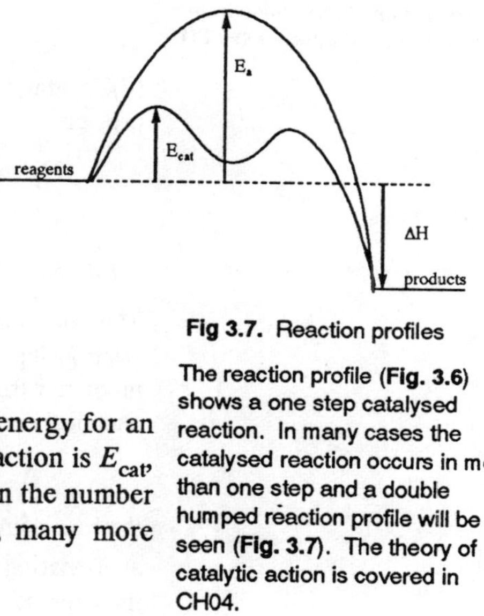

Fig 3.7. Reaction profiles

The reaction profile (**Fig. 3.6**) shows a one step catalysed reaction. In many cases the catalysed reaction occurs in more than one step and a double humped reaction profile will be seen (**Fig. 3.7**). The theory of catalytic action is covered in CH04.

The Maxwell-Boltzmann curve in Fig. 3.8, shows that, if the activation energy for an uncatalysed reaction is E_a, and the activation energy for a catalysed reaction is E_{cat}, the number of molecules with energy greater than E_{cat} is much larger than the number with energy greater than E_a. In the presence of a catalyst, therefore, many more particles have sufficient energy to react, and the rate is greatly increased.

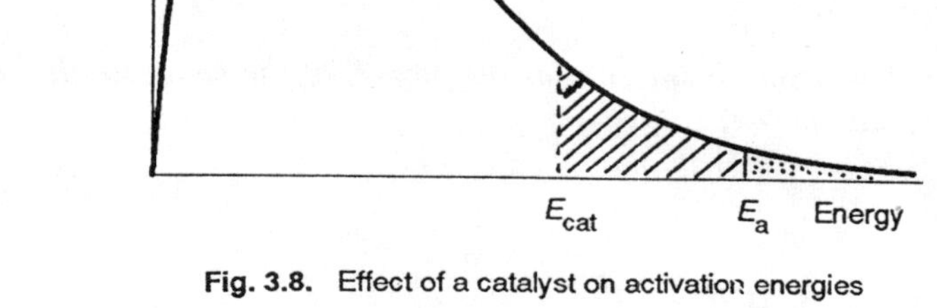

Fig. 3.8. Effect of a catalyst on activation energies

Types of catalyst
Catalysts can be in the same phase or physical state as the reagents (a homogeneous catalyst) or in a different phase (a heterogeneous catalyst).

Examples of homogeneous catalysts
(i) the use of acids to catalyse the formation (or hydrolysis) of esters, e.g. the formation of methyl ethanoate

$$CH_3COOH + CH_3OH \rightleftharpoons CH_3COOCH_3 + H_2O$$

(ii) the use of transition metal ions in solution to catalyse redox reactions, e.g. the oxidation of iodide ions by persulphate ions ($S_2O_8^{2-}$).

Transition metals make good catalysts for redox reactions as they can easily change their oxidation state. See 5.2.4 for further examples.

$$2I^- + S_2O_8^{2-} \rightarrow I_2 + 2SO_4^{2-}$$

This reaction is normally extremely slow, but Fe^{3+} ions catalyse the reaction in a two step process.

$$2Fe^{3+} + 2I^- \rightarrow 2Fe^{2+} + I_2$$

$$S_2O_8^{2-} + 2Fe^{2+} \rightarrow 2Fe^{3+} + 2SO_4^{2-}$$

Although the Fe^{3+} ions are reduced in the first step, they are reformed in the second step and so are not consumed overall, i.e. they are acting catalytically.

Examples of heterogeneous catalysts
Examples of this type include the catalysis of gas phase reactions on the surface of solid catalysts, such as
(i) the hydrogenation of alkenes such as ethene using nickel or platinum catalysts

The production of margarine from vegetable oils is discussed in 3.2.4.

$$C_2H_4 + H_2 \rightarrow C_2H_6$$

(ii) catalysis of the reaction between nitrogen and hydrogen by iron (the Haber process).

$$N_2 + 3H_2 \rightleftharpoons 2NH_3$$

3.1.4 Simple rate equations

The rate of a reaction depends on the concentration of the reagents involved. The exact relationship between the rate of reaction and the concentration, however, cannot be predicted from the overall chemical equation, e.g. for a reaction for which the overall chemical equation is

$$A + B \rightarrow C$$

the rate of reaction is not necessarily directly proportional to [A] or to [B] (where the abbreviation [A] is used to denote the concentration of A in mol dm^{-3}) but is given by the expression

$$\text{rate} \propto [A]^m [B]^n$$

The powers m and n are usually integral, most commonly 0, 1 or 2, and are described as the *orders* of reaction with respect to the reactants A and B.

If the expression is modified to become an equation, it is called a *rate equation* with a constant of proportionality, k, known as a *rate constant* or *velocity constant*. At a given temperature, k is constant so that

$$\text{rate} = k[A]^m [B]^n$$

The overall order of a reaction is the sum of the powers of the concentration terms in the rate equation, i.e. (m + n).

Zero order

Consider a reaction for which the rate equation is

rate = $k[A]^m$

If m is zero, in this equation, then

rate = k

i.e. the rate of reaction is constant and independent of the concentration of A. If the rate of reaction is constant (Fig. 3.9), a graph of [A] against time is a straight line (Fig. 3.10).

The units of a zero order rate constant are those of rate, e.g. mol dm^{-3} s^{-1}.

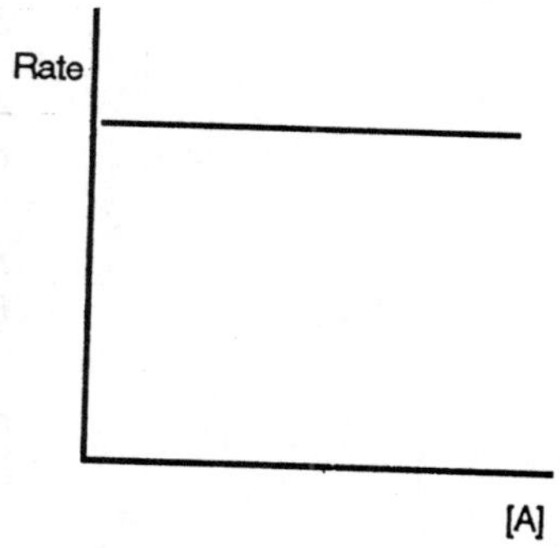

Fig. 3.9 Zero order

First order

If m is 1 in the above equation, the rate equation becomes

rate = $k[A]$

and the reaction is first order with respect to A. If [A] doubles, the rate doubles. Fig. 3.11 shows how concentration varies with time for a first order reaction.

If the rate has units mol dm^{-3} s^{-1}, the first order rate constant, k, has units s^{-1}.

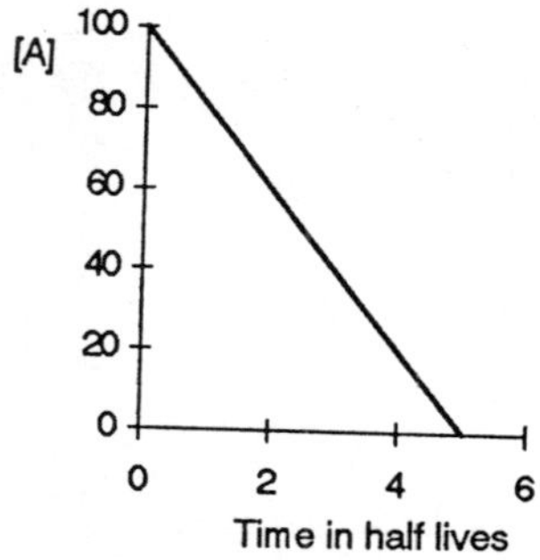

Fig. 3.10 Zero order

Second order

The rate equation for a second order reaction could be either

rate = $k[A]^2$, where the reaction is second order with respect to A, or

rate = $k[A][B]$, where the reaction is first order with respect both to A and to B and the overall order is (1 + 1) = 2.

Fig. 3.12 shows how concentration varies with time for a second order reaction.

A second order rate constant has units $\dfrac{\text{mol dm}^{-3}\ \text{s}^{-1}}{(\text{mol dm}^{-3})\ (\text{mol dm}^{-3})}$ = mol^{-1} dm^{+3} s^{-1}

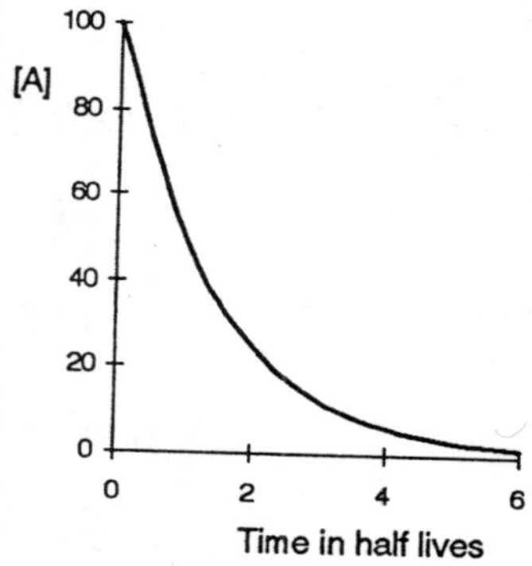

Fig. 3.11 First order

Third order

If m = 2 and n = 1 in the rate equation, then

rate = $k[A]^2$ [B] and the overall order is (2 + 1) = 3.

A third order rate constant has units $\dfrac{\text{mol dm}^{-3}\ \text{s}^{-1}}{(\text{mol dm}^{-3})^2 (\text{mol dm}^{-3})}$ = mol^{-2} dm^{+6} s^{-1}

Fourth order

If m = 2 and n = 2 in the rate equation, then

rate = $k[A]^2$ $[B]^2$ and the overall order is (2 + 2) = 4.

A fourth order rate constant has units $\dfrac{\text{mol dm}^{-3}\ \text{s}^{-1}}{(\text{mol dm}^{-3})^2 (\text{mol dm}^{-3})^2}$ = mol^{-3} dm^{+9} s^{-1}

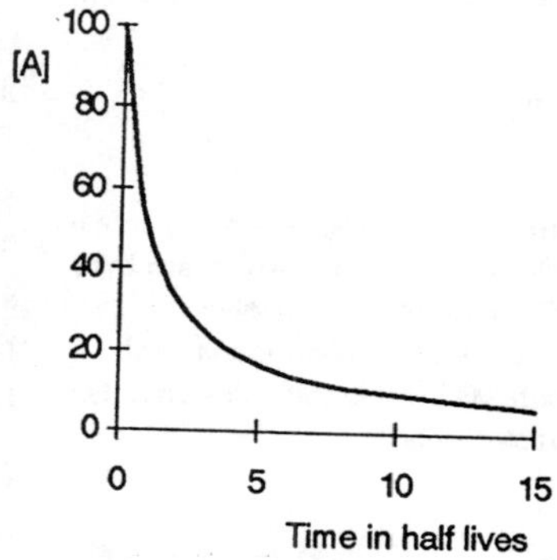

Fig. 3.12 Second order

Effect of temperature on the rate constant, k

An increase in temperature increases the rate of reaction. The rate constant k, also increases exponentially with increased temperature see Fig 3.13.

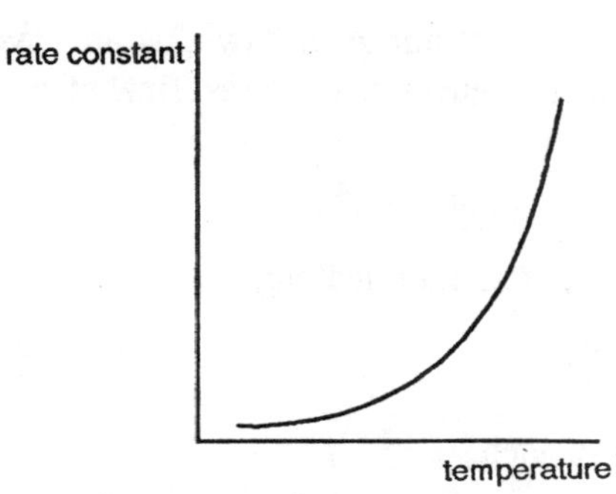

Fig. 3.13 Variation of rate constant with temperature

3.1.5 Determination of rate equations

As a reaction proceeds, the rate of reaction decreases since the concentration of the reagents falls as they are being used up. The rate at a particular time is found by measuring the gradient at that time on a graph of concentration against time, (see Fig. 3.3). The rate at the start of the reaction, when the initial concentrations of the reagents are exactly known, is called the ***initial rate.***

If the experiment is repeated several times using different initial concentrations of reagents, the initial rate changes. By studying the effect on the initial rate of changes in the initial concentrations of reagents, the rate equation can be derived.

Example 1: The following data were obtained for the reaction:

$$A + 3B \rightarrow AB_3$$

Experiment	Initial [A] /mol dm^{-3}	Initial [B] /mol dm^{-3}	Initial rate /mol dm^{-3} min^{-1}
1	0·100	0·100	0·002
2	0·100	0·200	0·008
3	0·100	0·300	0·018
4	0·200	0·100	0·004
5	0·300	0·100	0·006

If we consider experiments 1 and 2:
the concentration of A is kept constant and the concentration of B is doubled.
The rate increases by a factor of (0.008 / 0.002) = 4 or 2^2 i.e. rate $\propto [B]^2$
or the reaction is second order with respect to B.
To confirm this, use experiments 1 and 3:
the concentration of A is kept constant and the concentration of B is multiplied by 3.
The rate increases by a factor of (0.018 / 0.002) = 9 or 3^2, i.e. rate $\propto [B]^2$

If we consider experiments 1 and 4:
the concentration of A is doubled and the concentration of B is kept constant.
The rate increases by a factor of (0.004 / 0.001) = 2, i.e. rate $\propto$ [A]
or the reaction is first order with respect to A

Overall the rate $\propto [A][B]^2$ i.e. the overall order is 1 + 2 = 3
hence the rate equation is

The rate equation is derived from experimental results, it cannot be deduced from the overall equation.

rate = k $[A][B]^2$

Mechanisms

For any reaction which involves more than two species reacting, the chance of all the species colliding at the same instant is remote, therefore the reaction will proceed in a series of steps each usually involving a collision between two particles. One of these steps is slower than the others and is known as the *rate determining step*. The rate equation shows only those reagent species which are involved in the reaction sequence before and during rate determining step.

Three body collisions are extremely unlikely. Reactions which are third order or more must involve a sequence of reaction steps each of which will involve the collision of two particles only.

In the example above, the rate equation shows that one A and two Bs are involved in and before the rate determining step; the other B must react in a fast final step.
A possible reaction sequence could be:

Step 1 $B + B \rightarrow B_2$ (a dimer of B)

Step 2 $B_2 + A \rightarrow AB_2$ (an intermediate)

Step 3 $AB_2 + B \rightarrow AB_3$

Step 2 must be the slowest or rate determining step.

Example 2

The following data refer to the reaction:

$2P + Q \rightarrow R + S$

Experiment	Initial [P] /mol dm^{-3}	Initial [Q] /mol dm^{-3}	Initial rate /mol dm^{-3} s^{-1}
1	0.5	0.5	2×10^{-4}
2	1.0	0.5	8×10^{-4}
3	1.0	1.0	8×10^{-4}
4	1.5	1.5	18×10^{-4}

If we consider experiments 1 and 2:
the concentration of Q is kept constant and the concentration of P is doubled.
The rate increases by a factor of ($8 \times 10^{-4} / 2 \times 10^{-4}$) = 4 or 2^2, i.e. rate $\propto [P]^2$
or the reaction is second order with respect to P.

If we consider experiments 2 and 3:
the concentration of P is kept constant and the concentration of Q is doubled.
The rate is unchanged i.e. rate is independent of [Q] or the rate $\propto [Q]^0$
i.e. the reaction is zero order with respect to Q.

Overall the rate $\propto [P]^2$ i.e. the overall order is 2
hence the rate equation is

rate = k $[P]^2$

A possible mechanism could be:

Step 1 $P + P \rightarrow$ X (an intermediate)

Step 2 $X + Q \rightarrow R + S$

Step 1 must be the slowest step in the reaction, therefore, since this does not involve Q.

It is by consideration of kinetic data of this sort, that the mechanisms of reactions are deduced. Such information is important in deciding how to maximise the rate of a reaction, perhaps of an industrial process. Increasing the concentration of Q, for instance, in example 2 above would have no effect on the rate and would be a waste of money.

3.2 INTRODUCTION TO ORGANIC CHEMISTRY

3.2.1 Naming organic compounds

Organic chemistry is the study of the millions of covalent compounds of the element carbon. These compounds constitute an enormous range of materials with diverse properties which range from living systems to synthetic materials made from petroleum such as drugs, medicines, and plastics. In this module we shall consider mainly the chemistry of the molecules derived from the hydrocarbons present in petroleum.

Whenever a new compound is studied, traditionally it is first analysed to determine the percentage composition by mass of each element present. From this data, the empirical formula of the substance can be derived (see also 1.2.4)

The ***empirical formula*** shows the simplest ratio of atoms of each element present, e.g. a compound **X** is found to contain 40.0% carbon, 6.7% hydrogen, and 53.3% oxygen by mass.

	Carbon	Hydrogen	Oxygen
% by mass	40.0	6.7	53.3
Divide by Ar	40.0 / 12 = 3.33	6.7 / 1 = 6.7	53.3 / 16 = 3.33
Divide by the smallest	3.33 / 3.33 = 1	6.7 / 3.33 = 2	3.33 / 3.33 = 1
Simplest ratio	1	2	1

Empirical formula = CH_2O

The empirical formula for **X**, CH_2O, gives the simplest ratio of atoms, but this formula can represent many different molecules.

The ***molecular formula*** gives the actual number of atoms of each element present in a molecule and is a multiple of the empirical formula, i.e. $(CH_2O)_n$.

In order to discover the value of n in $(CH_2O)_n$, we need to know the molecular mass of the compound, **X**. The empirical formula, CH_2O, has mass 30. If the molecular mass is found to be 60, then the value of n is 2 and the molecular formula is $(CH_2O)_2$ which is more usually written as $C_2H_4O_2$.

The molecular formula can represent several compounds in which the two atoms of carbon, four atoms of hydrogen, and two atoms of oxygen are arranged differently. These molecules are called *isomers*.

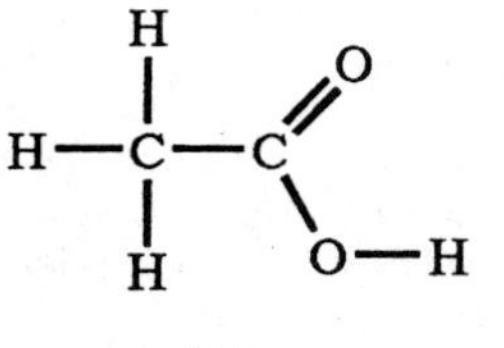

3.1

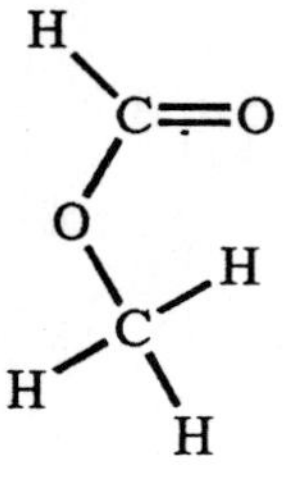

3.2

Structural isomerism

Compounds with the same molecular formula but different structures are known as *structural isomers*. The molecular formula for **X**, $C_2H_4O_2$, can represent ethanoic acid (**3.1**) and methyl methanoate (**3.2**) or other isomers.

Isomerism is considered in detail in section 3.2.10.

To avoid confusion between structural isomers, molecular formulae should not be used in equations. Equation 1 below is unambiguous whereas the compounds in equation 2 could be confused.

$$CH_3COOH + C_2H_5OH \rightarrow CH_3COOC_2H_5 + H_2O \quad \text{Equation 1}$$

$$C_2H_4O_2 + C_2H_6O \rightarrow C_4H_8O_2 + H_2O \quad \text{Equation 2}$$

To identify a compound exactly from the possible structural isomers, the properties of the compound need to be studied. Thus if **X** is found to be acidic, it will be ethanoic acid, CH_3COOH, rather than the neutral ester methyl methanoate, $HCOOCH_3$.

The representation of the two isomers by structural formulae, showing all the bonds present is itself an approximation since the molecules are 3-dimensional and not planar as they are represented on paper here. Full structural formulae, however, can be cumbersome to draw and usually a simplified or 'abbreviated' formula is used, e.g. ethyl ethanoate, $C_4H_8O_2$ is more simply written as $CH_3COOCH_2CH_3$ than the full structural formula (**3.3**).

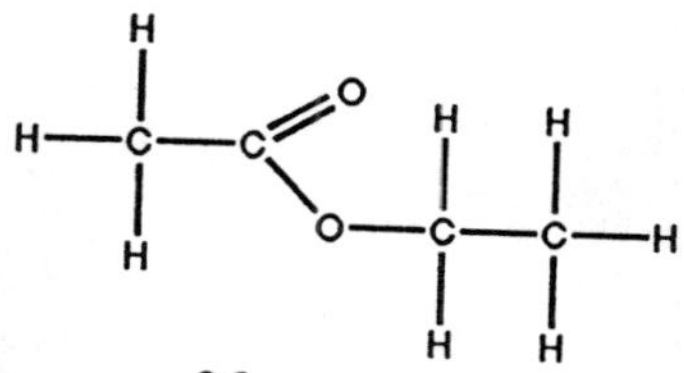

3.3

Nowadays this technique of analysis by finding empirical formula and molecular mass, followed by a study of the reactions of the substance to identify the functional group present, have been superseded by the instrumental methods of infra-red spectroscopy, nuclear magnetic resonance spectroscopy, and mass spectrometry. These more modern methods are considered in 3.2.11.

The organic compounds we shall consider are almost all based on the series of hydrocarbons called alkanes (see 3.2.3) with one of the hydrogen atoms replaced by an atom or group of atoms called a functional group.

The ***functional group*** is the reactive part of the molecule which largely determines the properties of the molecule. A family of molecules which all contain the same functional group is called an homologous series. Functional groups which appear in this module are given in Table 3.2.

An ***homologous series*** is a number of compounds which can all be represented by a general formula, e.g.

C_nH_{2n+2} represents the alkanes

C_nH_{2n} represents the alkenes

$C_nH_{2n+1}OH$ represents the alcohols

All members of the same series have similar chemical properties since these properties are determined by the functional group present; their physical properties show a gradual change as the carbon chain gets longer, e.g. the boiling points of the alkanes increase as the homologous series is ascended and the number of carbons increases.

Rules for naming organic compounds

Organic compounds are named according to the rules of the International Union of Pure and Applied Chemistry. These systematic or IUPAC names are based on those of the parent alkanes.

To assign a name, look first for the longest carbon chain; the number of carbons in this skeleton determines the stem of the name, (see Table 3. 1).

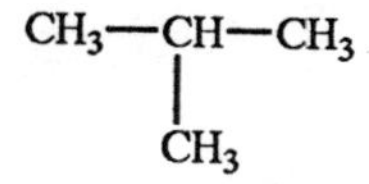

3.4

is called methylpropane as the longest chain has 3 carbon atoms (propane) with a one carbon branch (methyl).

Table 3.1 The first six alkanes

Number of carbon atoms	1	2	3	4	5	6
Name	methane	ethane	propane	butane	pentane	hexane
Formula	CH_4	C_2H_6	C_3H_8	C_4H_{10}	C_5H_{12}	C_6H_{14}

Branching

In many compounds the skeleton is branched. The names of the side chains also depend on the number of carbons so that

- a one carbon branch (CH_3) is called *methyl*
- a two carbon branch (CH_3CH_2) is called *ethyl*
- a three carbon branch ($CH_3CH_2CH_2$) is called *propyl*

Table 3.2 Homologous series and functional groups

Homologous series	Name: prefix or suffix	Functional group	Example
Alkanes	suffix -ane	C—H	ethane C_2H_6
Alkenes	suffix -ene	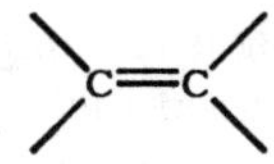	ethene C_2H_4
Haloalkanes	prefix chloro-	—Cl	chloroethane CH_3CH_2Cl
Alcohols	suffix -ol	—OH	ethanol CH_3CH_2OH
	prefix hydroxy-		2-hydroxypropanoic acid $CH_3CH(OH)COOH$
Aldehydes	suffix -al	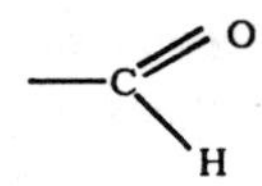	ethanal CH_3CHO
Ketones	suffix -one	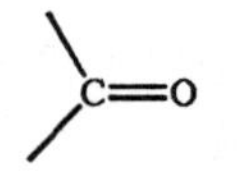	propanone CH_3COCH_3
	prefix oxo-		3-oxobutanoic acid CH_3COCH_2COOH
Carboxylic acids	suffix -oic acid	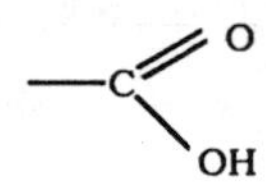	ethanoic acid CH_3COOH
Esters	suffix -oate	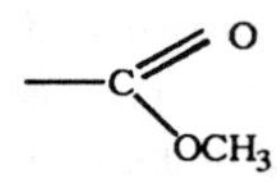	methyl ethanoate CH_3COOCH_3

Numbering of position

The position of any branch on the chain must also be made clear. This is achieved by numbering the carbons in the skeleton in such a way as to keep the numbers used as low as possible when indicating the position of any branches. For example, the molecule shown as **3.5**, is called 2-methylpentane (numbering from the right) and not 4-methylpentane (numbering from the left).

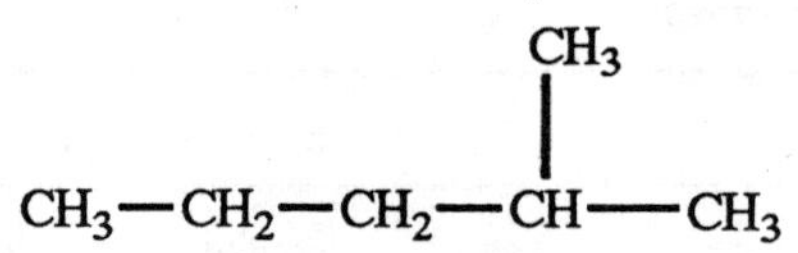

3.5

3.6

Note that these molecules are three dimensional and each carbon is surrounded tetrahedrally by four bonds with bond angles of 109½° (**3.6**). However, on paper it is usually simpler to represent a structure as if it had bond angles of 90° or 180°, i.e. the three structures given below are all 3-methylpentane. Always remember to look for the longest carbon chain when naming an organic molecule.

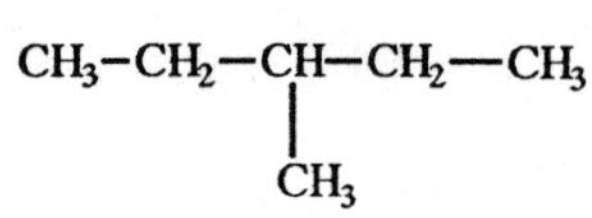

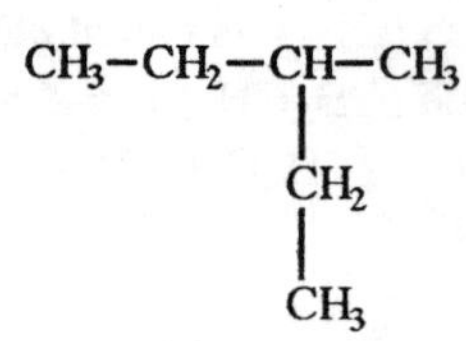

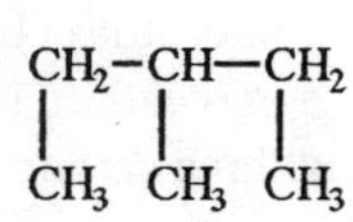

Functional groups

- The *type* of functional group present is indicated either by a prefix or a suffix on the alkane stem (see Table 3.2).
- The *position* of the functional group is indicated by a number, e.g. 2-chloropropane, (**3.7**) has the chlorine atom on the second (middle) carbon atom.

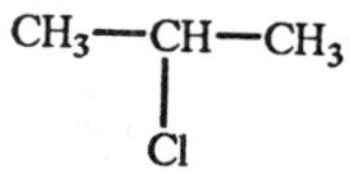

3.7

- For aldehydes and carboxylic acids the functional group must be on the end of the carbon chain. It is therefore automatically numbered as carbon-1 and the number need not be included in the name, e.g. propanal is CH_3CH_2CHO.
- When two or more of a particular functional group are present, the *number* of substituents is shown by using the prefixes di- for two, tri- for three or tetra- for four, e.g. dichloromethane, CH_2Cl_2, or tetrachloromethane, CCl_4.
- Numbers 1,2, etc. must also be used to show the position of *each* functional group. Commas are used between numbers and hyphens between numbers and letters, e.g.

  CH_3CCl_3 is called 1,1,1-trichloroethane and

  $HOCH_2CH_2OH$ is called ethane-1,2-diol

When naming compounds. Look for:
the longest carbon chain ?
functional group(s) ?
how many substituents ?
where are they ?

- If more than one type of functional group is present, their positions and names as prefixes are listed in alphabetical order, e.g.

  $CH_3CHBrCH_2Cl$ is 2-bromo-1-chloropropane

- Where two names which are usually suffixes are needed, the ending for acid takes precedence over aldehyde or ketone which takes precedence over alcohol, e.g.

  $CH_3CH(OH)COOH$ is 2-hydroxypropanoic acid and

  CH_3COCH_2COOH is 3-oxobutanoic acid.

Where names become very complicated, trivial names are often used, e.g. glucose (**3.9**) is one of the isomers of 2,3,4,5,6-pentahydroxyhexanal

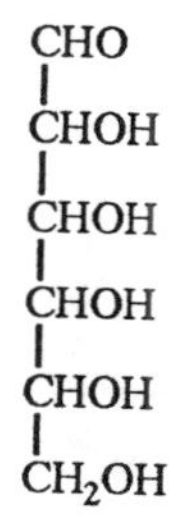

3.9

- The suffix -ene for alkenes can be placed in front of other suffixes, e.g.

  $H_2C = CH—CHCl—CHO$ is 2-chlorobut-3-enal and

  3.8 is 3,5-dichloro-4-hydroxy-2-methylhexanal (!)

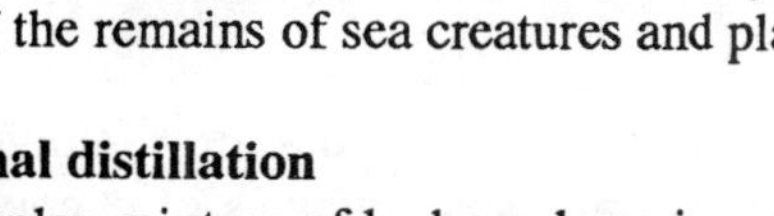

3.8

3.2.2 Petroleum: fractional distillation and cracking

Petroleum

Petroleum or crude oil is a mixture of hydrocarbons, mainly alkanes, formed by the decay of the remains of sea creatures and plants over millions of years.

Fractional distillation

The complex mixture of hydrocarbons is separated into smaller mixtures or fractions by fractional distillation (primary distillation).

The crude oil is heated and the vapour/liquid mixture passed into a tower. The top of the tower is cooler than the bottom; i.e. there is a temperature gradient. This separates the petroleum mixture into fractions depending on the boiling points of the hydrocarbons present. Only those with low boiling points reach the top. Others condense in trays at different levels up the tower and are drawn off there.

The residue from the primary distillation still contains useful material such as lubricating oil and waxes which boil above 350 °C at atmospheric pressure. At such high temperatures some of the components in the residue decompose so, to obtain these, the residue is further distilled but under reduced pressure (vacuum distillation). The reduced pressure lowers their boiling points so they can be distilled without decomposing.

The major fractions and their uses are shown in Table 3.3.

Table 3.3 Fractions from crude oil

Name of fraction	Boiling range (°C) (approx)	Uses	Length of carbon chain (approx)
LPG (Liquefied petroleum gas)	up to 25	calor gas; camping gaz	1 - 4
Petrol (gasoline)	40 - 100	petrol	4 - 12
Naphtha	100 - 150	petrochemicals	7 - 14
Kerosine (paraffin)	150 - 250	jet fuel petrochemicals	11 - 15
Gas oil (diesel)	220 - 350	central heating fuel petrochemicals	15 - 19
Mineral oil (lubricating oil)	over 350	lubricating oil petrochemicals	20 - 30
Fuel oil	over 400	fuel for ships and power stations	30 - 40
Wax, grease	over 400	candles, grease for bearings, polish	41 - 50
Bitumen	over 400	roofing; road surfacing	above 50

Petroleum is a mixture consisting mainly of alkanes hydrocarbons.

The composition of crude oil varies from place to place. In general, however, the amount of each fraction produced does not match the demand, see Table 3.4.

Table 3.4 Supply and demand for oil fractions

Fraction	Approximate % in Crude oil	Demand
Gases	2	4
Petrol and naphtha	16	27
Kerosine	13	8
Gas oil	19	23
Fuel oil and bitumen	50	38

We use a higher proportion of the high value products such as petrol than occurs naturally but have some of the heavier fractions to spare. To solve this imbalance, larger alkane molecules are broken up into smaller molecules in a process called *cracking*.

Cracking

In this process carbon-carbon and carbon-hydrogen bonds are split homolytically in free-radical reactions. Such reactions require considerable amounts of energy so high temperatures of about 800 °C are needed (*thermal* cracking). By using a silica/alumina catalyst, lower temperatures of about 450 °C can be used (*catalytic* cracking).

Large alkanes are cracked to form the smaller alkanes required for petrol together with alkenes, especially ethene, and hydrogen.

High M_r alkanes → smaller M_r alkanes + alkenes (mainly ethene) + hydrogen

When cracked, a molecule may break up in several different ways forming a mixture of products which can be separated by fractional distillation, e.g.

$$C_{14}H_{30} \rightarrow C_{10}H_{22} + 2C_2H_4 \quad \text{or}$$

$$C_{14}H_{30} \rightarrow C_{12}H_{24} + C_2H_4 + H_2$$

3.2.3 Alkanes: Combustion and chlorination

The alkanes are the homologous series of saturated hydrocarbons with the general formula C_nH_{2n+2}. The names of most organic compounds are based on those of the alkanes. The first six alkanes are listed in Table 3.1.

The lower alkanes are gases at room temperature. Their boiling points increase as the number of carbon atoms and hence the strength of the van der Waals' forces between the molecules increases. This increase in boiling points allows crude oil, a mixture consisting mainly of alkanes, to be separated by fractional distillation (see 3.2.2).

Combustion

Alkanes contain only carbon-carbon and carbon-hydrogen bonds. These are relatively strong bonds and are non-polar. Therefore alkanes are unreactive with acids, alkalis, electrophiles, and nucleophiles. In common with all hydrocarbons, however, they burn in air or oxygen in very exothermic reactions. Hence their important use as fuels.

In the presence of a plentiful supply of oxygen, *complete combustion* of alkanes occurs to form carbon dioxide and water: e.g.

Complete combustion of hydrocarbons produces carbon dioxide and water.

$$CH_4 + 2O_2 \rightarrow CO_2 + 2H_2O \qquad \Delta H^\circ = -890\ \text{kJ mol}^{-1}$$

$$C_4H_{10} + 6\tfrac{1}{2}O_2 \rightarrow 4CO_2 + 5H_2O \qquad \Delta H^\circ = -2880\ \text{kJ mol}^{-1}$$

As the number of carbons increases, more oxygen is required per mole of hydrocarbon for complete combustion.

If insufficient oxygen is available, *incomplete combustion* occurs and water is formed with either carbon monoxide or carbon. If, for example, a Bunsen burner is used with the air hole closed, the flame, instead of being blue, is yellow and luminous because of carbon particles in the flame. Any apparatus heated in a luminous flame becomes coated in black soot.

$$CH_4 + O_2 \rightarrow C + 2H_2O$$

Incomplete combustion forming carbon monoxide is, however, much more of a problem. Badly maintained gas central heating boilers which produce carbon monoxide because of an inadequate supply of air are an all too common cause of death by carbon monoxide poisoning.

$$CH_4 + 1\tfrac{1}{2}O_2 \rightarrow CO + 2H_2O$$

Internal combustion engines

Carbon monoxide is also formed by the incomplete combustion of petrol vapour in a car engine.

Cars with petrol engines produce carbon monoxide but diesel engines produce carbon and not carbon monoxide.

$$C_8H_{18} + 8\tfrac{1}{2}O_2 \rightarrow 8CO + 9H_2O$$

Such engines produce other pollutants, notably oxides of nitrogen, unburned hydrocarbons and, where leaded petrol is used, compounds of lead.

Oxides of nitrogen are also formed when the air/petrol mixture is sparked. The temperature can reach values of 2500 °C and this provides sufficient activation energy for nitrogen to react with oxygen forming nitrogen monoxide.

$$N_2 + O_2 \rightarrow 2NO$$

Nitrogen monoxide easily reacts with more oxygen to form nitrogen dioxide. With water and more oxygen, nitric acid is formed which can lead to acid rain.

$$2NO + O_2 \rightarrow 2NO_2$$

$$4NO_2 + 2H_2O + O_2 \rightarrow 4HNO_3$$

Nitrogen dioxide also reacts with oxygen or hydrocarbons in the presence of sunlight to form an irritating photochemical smog.

Catalytic converters

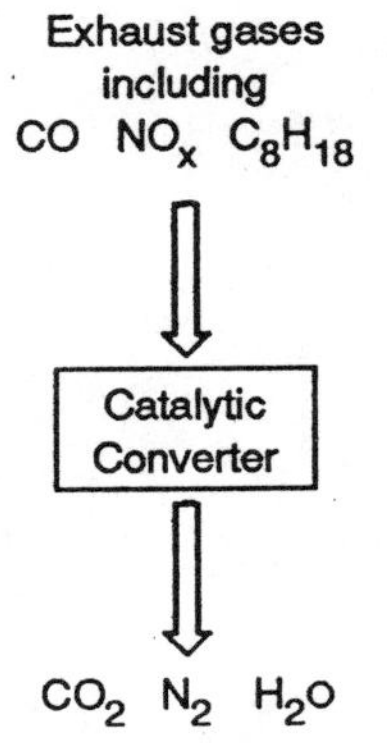

These help to remove the harmful gases from car exhausts. The converter contains a honeycomb of ceramic onto which metals such as platinum, palladium, and rhodium are spread in a thin layer. The metals catalyse reactions between the pollutants and help to remove up to 90% of the harmful gases, e.g.

$$2CO + 2NO \rightarrow 2CO_2 + N_2$$

$$C_8H_{18} + 25NO \rightarrow 8CO_2 + 12\tfrac{1}{2}N_2 + 9H_2O$$

Overall, the pollutant gases CO, NO_x and hydrocarbons are replaced by the harmless products CO_2, N_2, and H_2O.

Chlorination of methane

Methane does not react with chlorine at room temperature or in the dark. In the presence of ultraviolet light, however, a mixture of methane and chlorine will explode forming hydrogen chloride and a mixture of chlorinated methanes.

This is a ***free-radical substitution*** and the reaction occurs in several steps.

1 *Initiation*

$$Cl_2 \rightarrow 2Cl\cdot$$

The ultraviolet light provides the energy needed to start the reaction, i.e. to split some chlorine molecules into atoms (radicals). This occurs first as the Cl-Cl bond in chlorine is weaker than the C-H bond in methane.

2 *Propagation*

$$Cl\cdot + CH_4 \rightarrow CH_3\cdot + HCl$$

$$CH_3\cdot + Cl_2 \rightarrow CH_3Cl + Cl\cdot$$

In each step a radical is used and a radical is formed so the process continues and leads to a chain reaction. Each step is exothermic so the chain reaction can produce an explosion.

The overall reaction, which is the sum of the two propagation steps, can be represented by the equation

$$CH_4 + Cl_2 \rightarrow CH_3Cl + HCl$$

3 *Termination*

If two radicals combine they form a stable molecule and the sequence of reactions stops. Possible termination steps are

$$Cl\cdot + CH_3\cdot \rightarrow CH_3Cl \quad \text{and}$$

$$CH_3\cdot + CH_3\cdot \rightarrow CH_3CH_3$$

Chlorination of propane produces two monochloropropanes, 1-chloropropane and 2-chloropropane in an approximate ratio of 3 : 1 because of the ratio of 6 CH_3 hydrogens to 2 CH_2 hydrogens in propane.

Such termination steps lead to trace amounts of impurities, such as ethane, in the chloromethane.

Further substitution

The reaction of a chlorine radical with methane extracts a hydrogen radical to form HCl. Chloromethane still contains three hydrogen atoms so further pairs of propagation steps are possible leading to dichloromethane, CH_2Cl_2, trichloromethane $CHCl_3$, and finally tetrachloromethane, CCl_4, e.g.

$$Cl\cdot + CH_3Cl \rightarrow CH_2Cl\cdot + HCl$$

$$CH_2Cl\cdot + Cl_2 \rightarrow CH_2Cl_2 + Cl\cdot$$

The likelihood of further substitution can be reduced if an excess of methane is used.

3.2.4 Alkenes: structure and reactions

The alkenes are a homologous series of hydrocarbons with the general formula C_nH_{2n}. The first three members are

- ethene C_2H_4
- propene C_3H_6
- butene C_4H_8

The general formula for alkenes, C_nH_{2n}, can also represent a cyclic alkane, e.g. C_6H_{12} can represent several isomeric hexenes but also cyclohexane.

Alkenes contain two hydrogen atoms fewer than their parent alkane and are said to be unsaturated. This is because they contain a double bond between two carbon atoms. This bond is an area of high electron density and the cause of the high reactivity of alkenes.

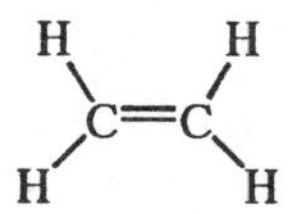

Ethene

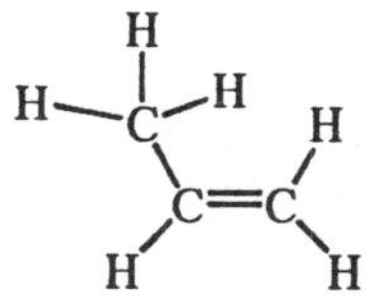

Propene

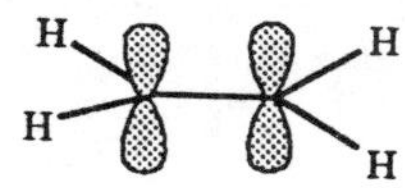

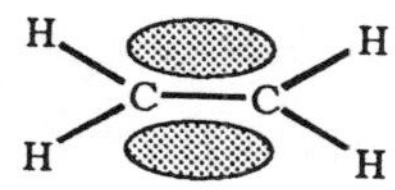

The double bond results from overlap of the spare p-orbital present on each carbon atom in the bond. This overlap produces a cloud of electrons above and below the molecule. The two carbon atoms of the double bond plus the four atoms attached to the double bond must lie in the same plane, i.e. ethene is a planar molecule.

Addition reactions

Alkenes can become saturated by the addition of small molecules across the double bond. In these reactions the double bond becomes a single carbon-carbon bond.

(a) with hydrogen (hydrogenation)

Alkenes react with hydrogen in the presence of a finely divided nickel catalyst at about 150 °C to form alkanes.

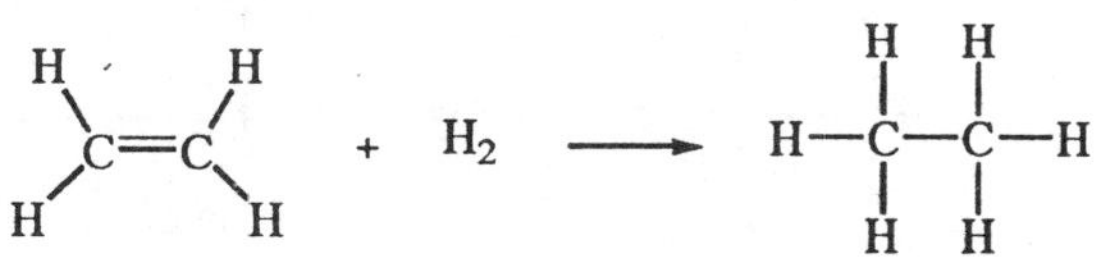

Ethane

Vegetable oils, which are mainly unsaturated compounds, are hardened in this way during the manufacture of margarines. The polyunsaturated liquid oils are partly saturated by reaction with hydrogen in the presence of a nickel catalyst to form solid fats. The amount of hydrogenation can be controlled so hard or soft margarines are produced as required.

The amount of unsaturation in a margarine or butter can be found by dissolving a sample in hexane and adding drops of bromine (*Toxic* and *Corrosive*). A surprisingly large amount of bromine is needed for butter.

(b) Electrophilic additions with

(i) bromine

Alkenes react with bromine to form a saturated, colourless product, e.g.

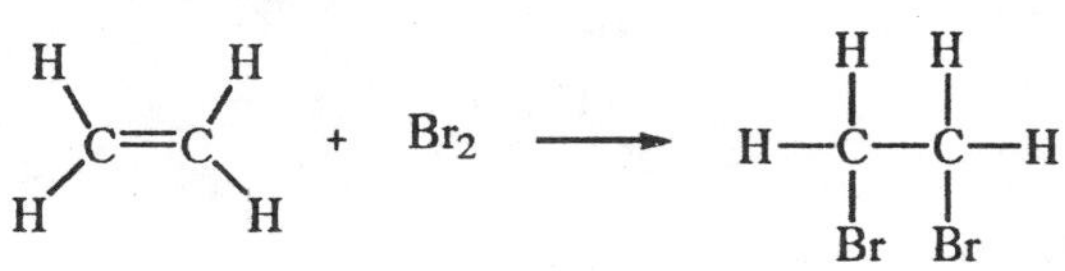

1,2-Dibromoethane

A solution of bromine in an organic solvent is decolourised by an alkene. This reaction is used as a test for unsaturation i.e. to distinguish alkenes from alkanes which do not react.

The mechanism of this reaction is ***electrophilic addition***:

- The electron rich area of the double bond induces a dipole in the bromine molecule. The electron deficient or δ+ bromine atom is the electrophile (*electron seeking species*)
- Electrons from the double bond form a new bond with the δ+ bromine and the other carbon in the double bond becomes an electron deficient carbonium ion. The bromine-bromine bond also breaks releasing a bromide ion.
- This bromide ion uses a lone pair of electrons to form a bond with the carbonium ion.
- The overall process involves addition across a carbon-carbon double bond.

The mechanism of electrophilic addition will only be required for symmetrical alkenes in CH03. The relative stabilities of carbonium ions are considered in CH06

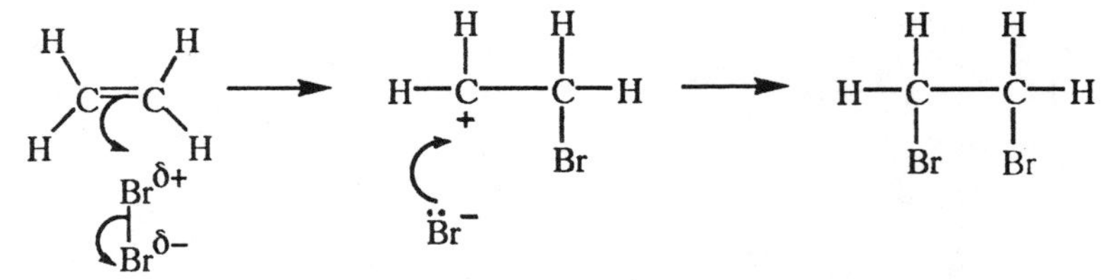

(ii) hydrogen bromide

Alkenes react with hydrogen bromide either in the gas phase or in concentrated aqueous solution to form bromoalkanes. e.g.

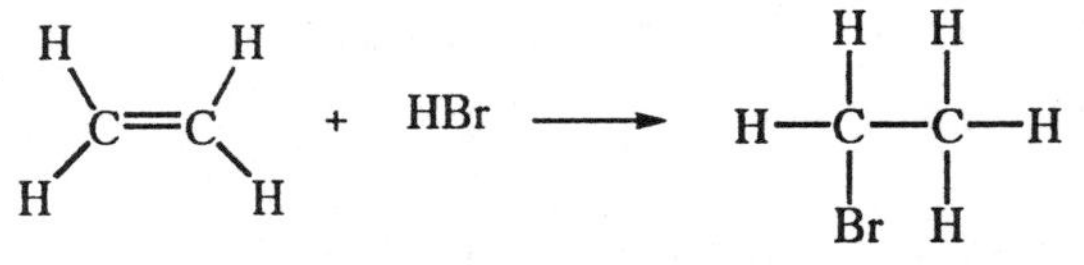

Bromoethane

The mechanism is similar except that H-Br possesses a permanent dipole; the hydrogen atom is electron deficient. If the reaction is performed in aqueous solution, $H^+(aq)$ ions act as electrophiles.

Note that a curly arrow represents the movement of a pair of electrons.

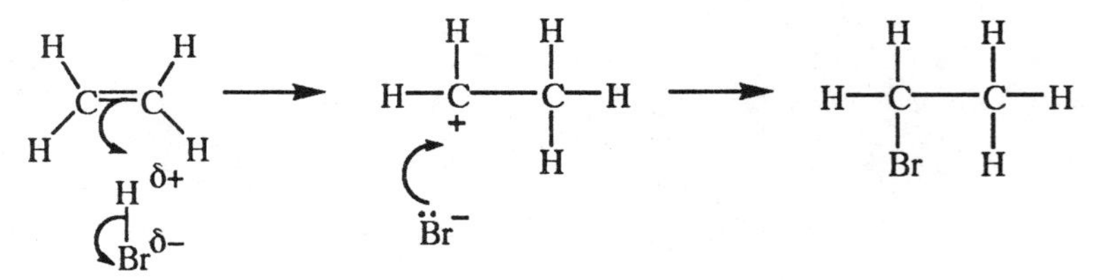

(iii) water (hydration)

Ethene reacts with steam at a temperature of 300 °C, a pressure of 6.5×10^3 kPa (65 atmospheres) and in the presence of phosphoric acid as catalyst, to form ethanol (see 3.2.7).

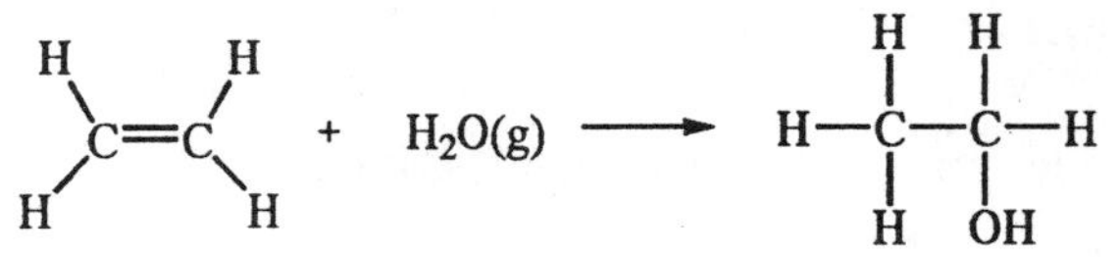

Ethanol

(c) Polymerisation (self addition)

Ethene molecules link together in the presence of a catalyst to form addition polymers which are saturated, e.g. poly(ethene).

The bond energies of C=C and C-C are 612 and 348 kJ mol^{-1} respectively. Polymerisation, i.e. forming two C-C bonds from one C=C bond, is therefore an exothermic process.

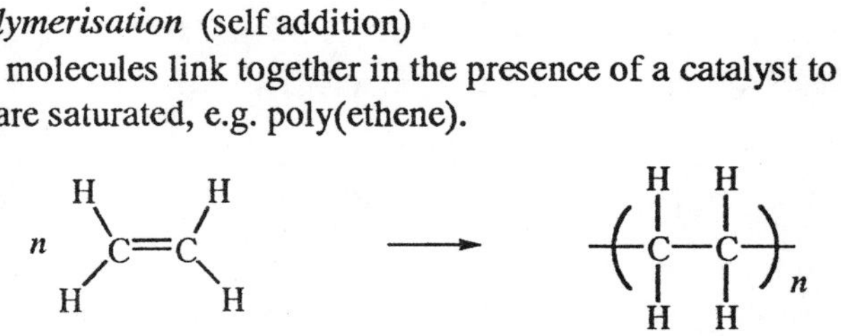

Poly(ethene)

Many polymers, including poly(propene) (**3.10**), poly(chloroethene) [or *PVC* from *poly(vinyl chloride)*] (**3.11**), and poly(phenylethene) (*polystyrene*) (**3.12**), can be formed from monomers where some or all of the hydrogens in ethene have been replaced by other atoms or groups of atoms.

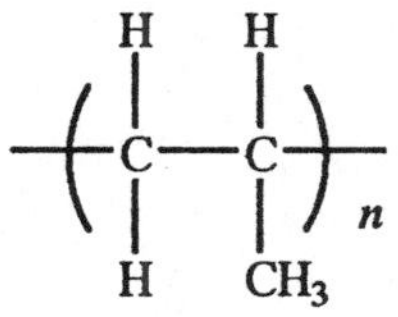

3.10

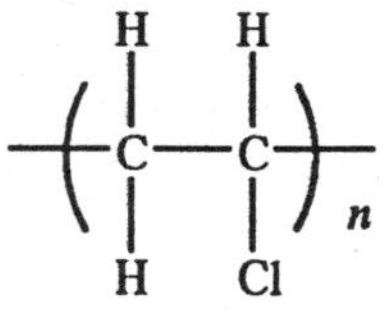

3.11

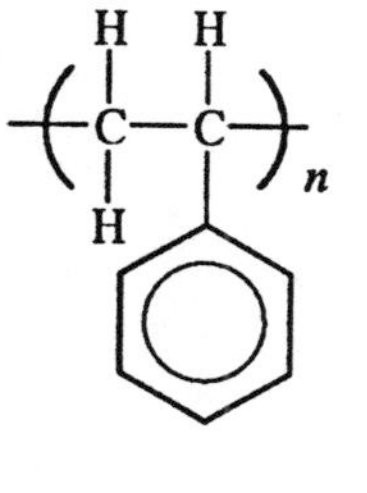

3.12

The repeating unit of the polymer should be drawn clearly from a given monomer, e.g.

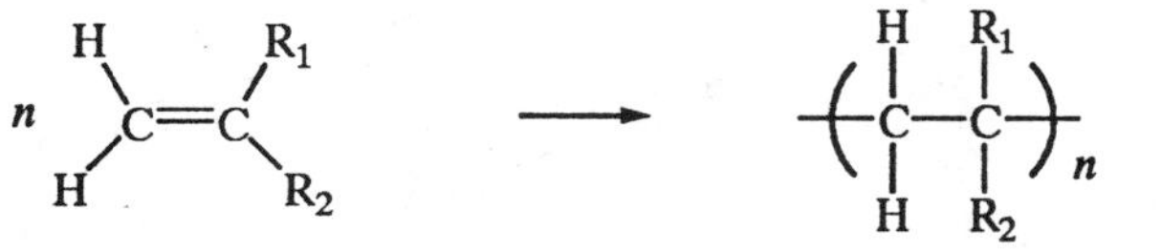

Monomer — Repeating unit

3.2.5 Aromatic Chemistry

Benzene, C_6H_6, is an aromatic hydrocarbon. Originally the term *aromatic* was used to refer to substances which had pleasant smells, but nowadays it means compounds, often called arenes, which are based on a benzene ring structure. Many aromatic compounds, in fact, have unpleasant odours.

The structure of benzene

Although the molecular formula of benzene had been known for over thirty years it was not until 1865 that Kekulé suggested a ring structure of alternate single and double bonds (**3.13**).

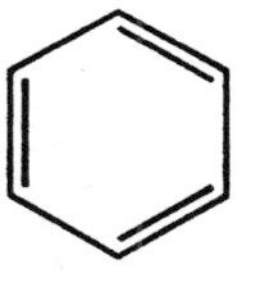

3.13

Although this cyclohexatriene structure can explain many of the properties of benzene, it could not explain the subsequent X-ray diffraction experiments which showed that the molecule is planar and that all the carbon-carbon bonds are the same length. It could also not explain that there is only one form of the compound 1,2-dibromobenzene and not the two shown as **3.14**.

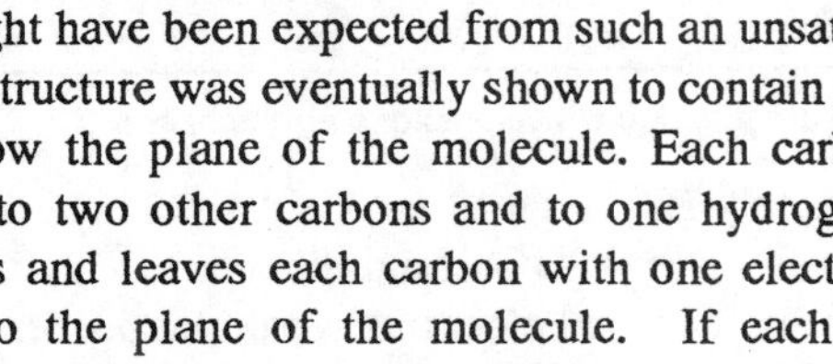

3.14

Benzene also shows few of the normal properties of alkenes, e.g. it has no reaction with solutions of bromine which alkenes would decolourise, and it is far less reactive than might have been expected from such an unsaturated molecule.

The structure was eventually shown to contain a ring of delocalised electrons above and below the plane of the molecule. Each carbon atom in the ring is covalently bonded to two other carbons and to one hydrogen atom. This bonding uses three electrons and leaves each carbon with one electron in a p-orbital which is at right angles to the plane of the molecule. If each p-orbital overlaps with one other p-orbital, the Kekulé structure of localised double bonds would be formed. However, if the p-orbitals overlap with both of their neighbours, a delocalised ring of electron density is formed (a π electron cloud above and below the plane of the ring). In the resulting hexagonal structure, all six carbon-carbon bonds are identical and of a length which is intermediate between that of a single and a double bond. This benzene structure is usually represented as **3.15**.

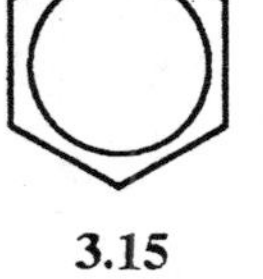

3.15

Thermochemical evidence of stability of benzene

The stability that the delocalised electrons confer on benzene can be seen from its enthalpy of hydrogenation, i.e. the enthalpy change when one mole of unsaturated compound reacts completely with hydrogen.

The enthalpy of hydrogenation of cyclohexene is -120 kJ mol^{-1}.

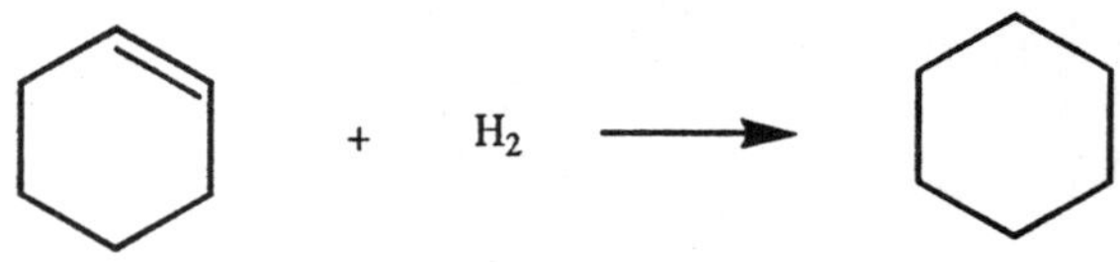

If benzene contained three carbon-carbon double bonds, we would expect that the enthalpy change for cyclohexatriene would be three times this, i.e. -360 kJ mol^{-1}.

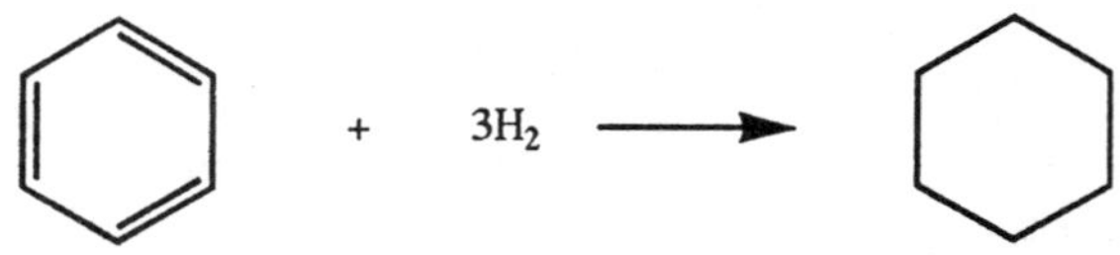

The enthalpy of hydrogenation of benzene is actually -208 kJ mol^{-1}.

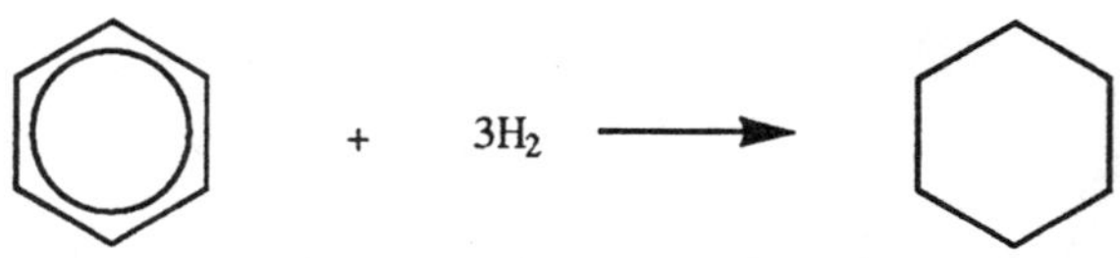

Therefore, benzene in releasing less energy on hydrogenation to form cyclohexane must normally be lower in energy than cyclohexatriene by *152 kJ* mol^{-1}.
This energy is known as the *delocalisation energy* of benzene (see Fig 3.14)

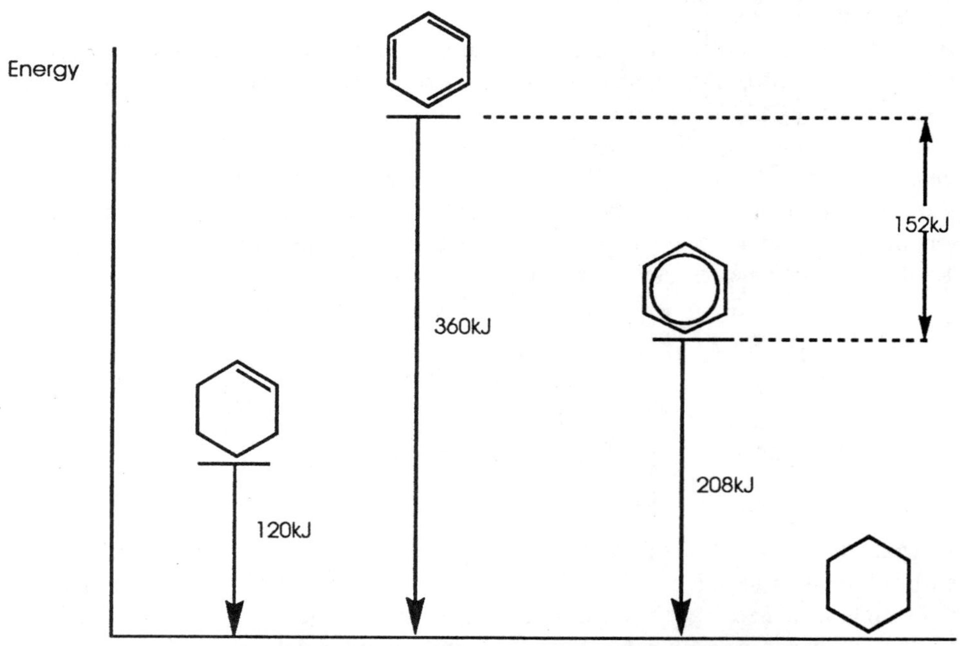

Fig. 3.14 Hydrogenation of cyclohexene and benzene

The delocalisation energy of approximately 150 kJ mol^{-1} not only gives benzene extra stability, but effectively prevents it from acting as a normal alkene. If addition did occur such as to form **3.16**, the ring of delocalised electrons would be broken. This would require far too much activation energy.

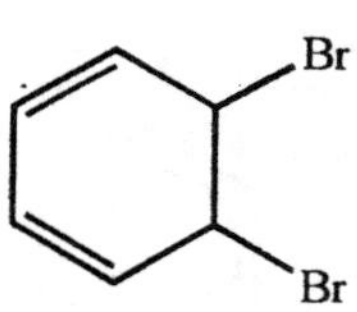

3.16

Addition to benzene does occur but such reactions require vigorous conditions and usually result in complete addition to give a saturated product, e.g. the hydrogenation reaction of benzene above forms only cyclohexane and requires heating to 150 °C in the presence of a catalyst such as nickel.

Electrophilic substitution

In its reactions, benzene keeps the π -electron cloud complete by undergoing substitution reactions. The delocalised electrons attract positive, i.e. electron-deficient species which are known as electrophiles. The most common reactions of benzene and other aromatic compounds (arenes) are therefore electrophilic substitutions, e.g. the nitration of benzene to form nitrobenzene in which benzene is heated to 50 °C with a mixture of concentrated nitric and concentrated sulphuric acids.

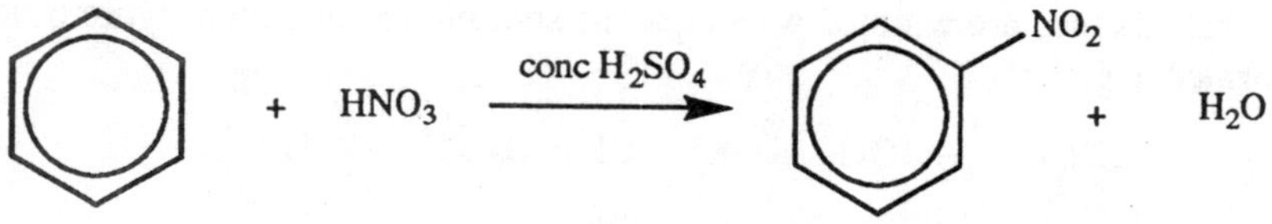

nitrobenzene

Nitrobenzene is an important intermediate in the production of many aromatic compounds notably phenylamine, $C_6H_5NH_2$ which is used in the preparation of dyes.

Concentrated sulphuric acid reacts with concentrated nitric acid to form the nitronium ion, NO_2^+, which is the electrophile in the substitution.

$$HNO_3 \quad + \quad 2H_2SO_4 \quad \rightleftharpoons \quad NO_2^+ \quad + \quad 2HSO_4^- \quad + \quad H_3O^+$$

The nitronium ion is attracted to the electron-rich ring and a bond is formed from a carbon in the ring to the nitrogen. This process disrupts the delocalised ring and forms an unstable cation. This intermediate rapidly loses a proton to reform the delocalised ring of electrons.

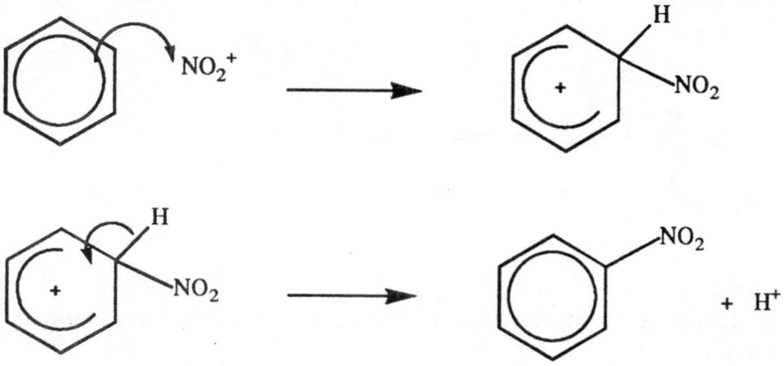

The mechanism of the nitration of benzene is not required in CH03. This and other electrophilic substitutions are considered in 6.1.2.

3.2.6 Haloalkanes and nucleophilic substitution

The haloalkanes are a homologous series of compounds with the general formula $C_nH_{2n+1}X$ where X is a halogen, i.e. F, Cl, Br, or I. e.g.

- CH_3CH_2Cl chloroethane
- $CH_3CHBrCH_3$ 2-bromopropane

Halogens atoms are very electronegative (see Table 3.5) so carbon-halogen bonds are polar. The electrons in the C-X bond are attracted towards the halogen atom which becomes δ–, leaving the carbon atom electron deficient or δ+.

The δ+ carbon is then susceptible to attack by nucleophiles, i.e. ions or molecules with a lone pair of electrons. When nucleophilic attack occurs, the carbon-halogen bond breaks and a halide ion is released. The nucleophile replaces the halogen atom in a nucleophilic substitution reaction, i.e.

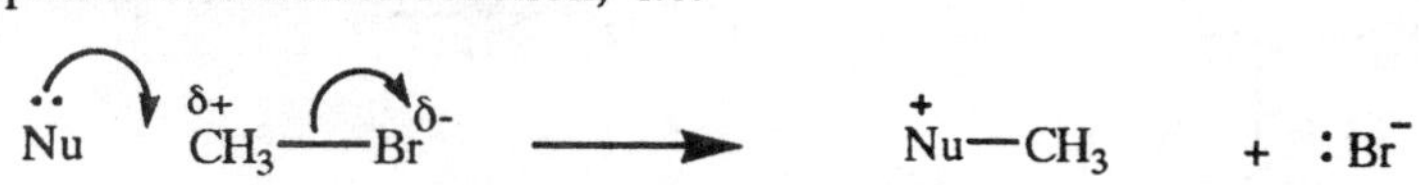

Table 3.5 Electronegativity values

Element	Electronegativity
C	2.5
F	4.0
Cl	3.0
Br	2.8
I	2.5

The rate of such reactions depends on the strength of the carbon-halogen bond: (see Table 3.6) Fluoroalkanes are very unreactive, because the C-F bond is so strong; chloroalkanes are also fairly slow to react. Carbon-bromine bonds, however, are more easily broken so bromoalkanes react at a reasonable rate.

Table 3.6 Carbon-halogen bond strengths

Bond	C-F	C-Cl	C-Br	C-I
Bond strength /kJ mol^{-1}	484	338	276	238

Examples of nucleophilic substitution reactions with

(i) hydroxide ions

When haloalkanes are warmed with aqueous sodium or potassium hydroxide, alcohols are formed, e.g.

$$CH_3CH_2Br + OH^- \rightarrow CH_3CH_2OH + Br^-$$

Ethanol

Elimination from haloalkanes, using for example hot ethanolic KOH, is not required in CH03, see 6.3.

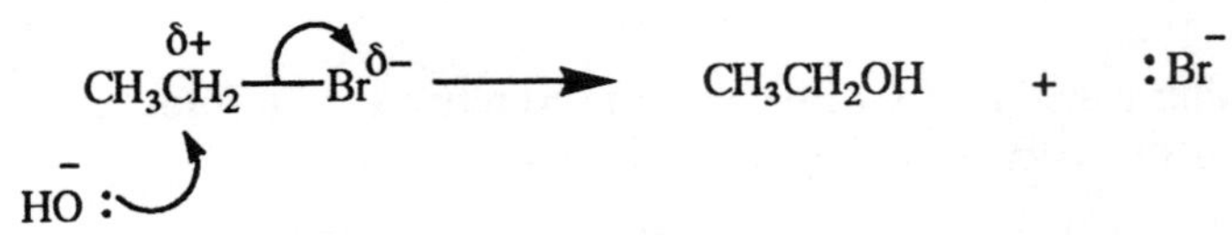

(ii) cyanide ions

When haloalkanes are warmed with aqueous/alcoholic solutions of potassium cyanide, nitriles are formed, e.g.

$$CH_3CH_2Br + CN^- \rightarrow CH_3CH_2CN + Br^-$$

Propanenitrile

Nucleophilic substitution with cyanide ions adds an extra carbon atom to the chain.

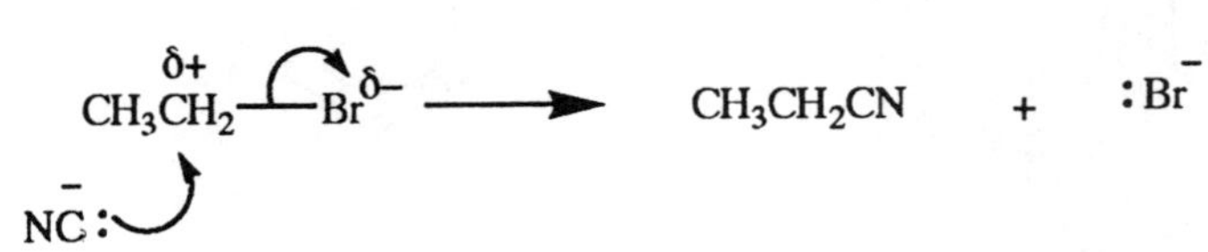

(iii) ammonia

When haloalkanes are warmed with an excess of ammonia, primary amines are formed, e.g. ethylamine.

$$CH_3CH_2Br + NH_3 \rightarrow CH_3CH_2NH_2 + HBr$$

Since the acid HBr will immediately react with the base ammonia, this equation is better written as

$$CH_3CH_2Br + 2\,NH_3 \rightarrow CH_3CH_2NH_2 + NH_4Br$$

Ethylamine

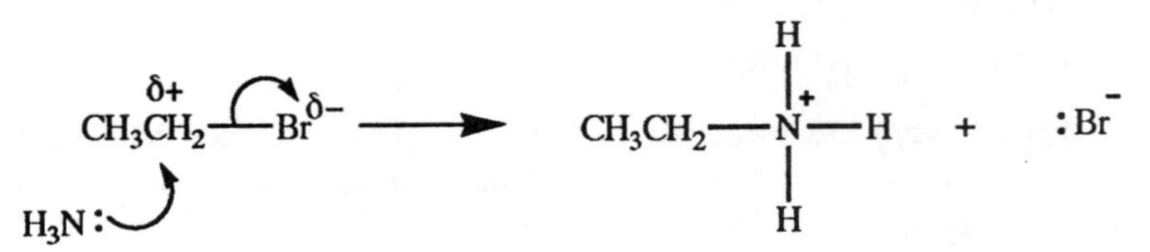

Reduction of nitriles, using hydrogen in the presence of a nickel catalyst, also forms primary amines.

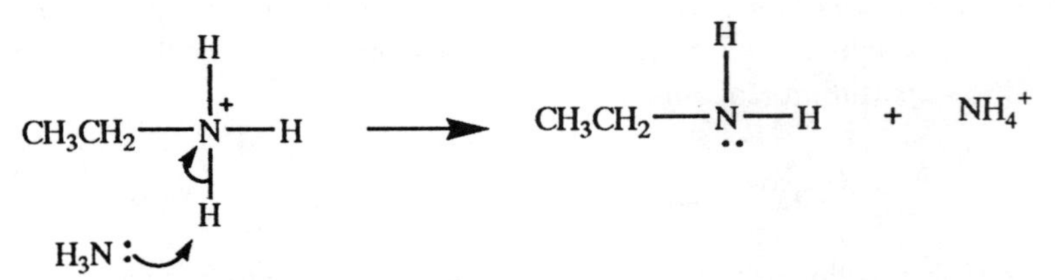

The excess of ammonia minimises the chance of further reaction of the primary amines to form secondary or tertiary amines or quaternary ammonium salts (see 6.2.2).

3.2.7 Alcohols

The alcohols are a homologous series with the general formula $C_nH_{2n+1}OH$. They all contain the functional group -OH which is called the hydroxyl group.
The first two alcohols are

- methanol CH_3OH
- ethanol CH_3CH_2OH

The most common alcohol is ethanol which is present in 'alcoholic' drinks.

Production of ethanol

(i) by fermentation

Alcohol is produced by the process called fermentation which uses living yeast cells to convert sugars such as glucose into carbon dioxide and ethanol.

$$C_6H_{12}O_6 \xrightarrow{\text{yeast}} 2C_2H_5OH + 2CO_2$$

Fermentation produces an aqueous solution of ethanol of concentration between 5 and 15%. Beers are usually about 5-7% and wines about 12%. Fermentation rarely produces higher ethanol concentrations since these kill the yeast. More concentrated solutions of alcohol, i.e. spirits such as whisky, brandy, or gin, which are about 40% ethanol, are made by fractional distillation of the fermented products.

The reaction is slow at low temperatures as the enzymes (natural catalysts) in yeast are inactivated. At higher temperatures the yeast is killed as the enzymes are denatured. The process is therefore normally carried out at about 35 °C.

(ii) by direct hydration

Ethanol is also produced industrially by the direct hydration of ethene using steam and a phosphoric acid catalyst at 300 °C and 6.5 x 10^3 kPa (65 atmospheres) pressure.

$$C_2H_4(g) + H_2O(g) \rightleftharpoons C_2H_5OH(g)$$

The direct hydration method is preferred at present for the production of ethanol for industrial use in the U.K. However, as this method uses ethene as a raw material, it may become less popular with respect to fermentation in the future when oil supplies begin to run out. Table 3.7 compares the two methods of production.

Table 3.7 Comparison of methods to produce ethanol

Method	Rate of reaction	Quality of product	Raw material	Type of process
Hydration	fast	pure	ethene from oil (a finite resource)	continuous (cheap on manpower)
Fermentation	slow	impure	sugars (a renewable resource)	batch (expensive on manpower)

Primary, secondary, and tertiary alcohols

Alcohols can be classified as primary, secondary or tertiary depending on the carbon skeleton to which the hydroxyl group is attached, (R = any alkyl or aryl group).

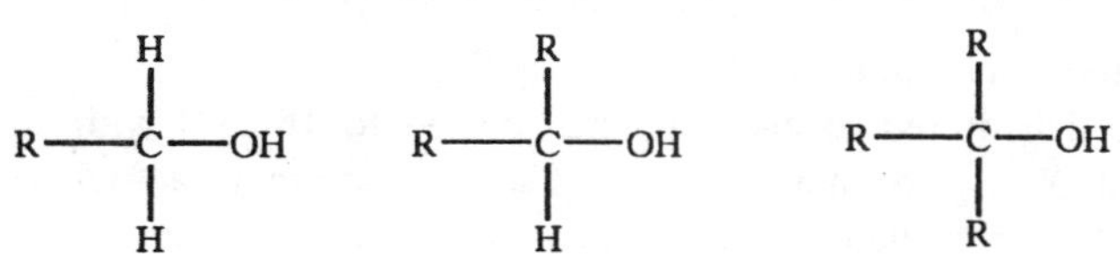

primary secondary tertiary

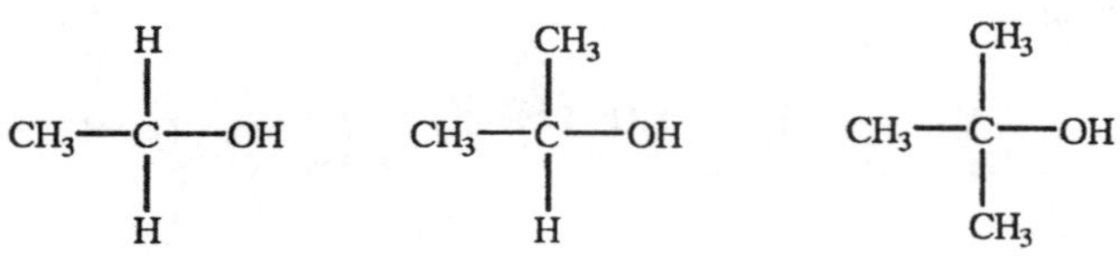

Ethanol	Propan-2-ol	2-Methylpropan-2-ol
primary	secondary	tertiary
I° or 1°	II° or 2°	III° or 3°

Many reactions of the OH functional group are the same, independent of where in a carbon skeleton the OH group is attached. However, the three types of alcohol differ in their reactions with oxidising agents such as acidified potassium dichromate(VI).

Oxidation of Alcohols

Primary alcohols are oxidised first to aldehydes such as ethanal.

The use of [O] to represent the oxidant is an allowed simplification in this case.

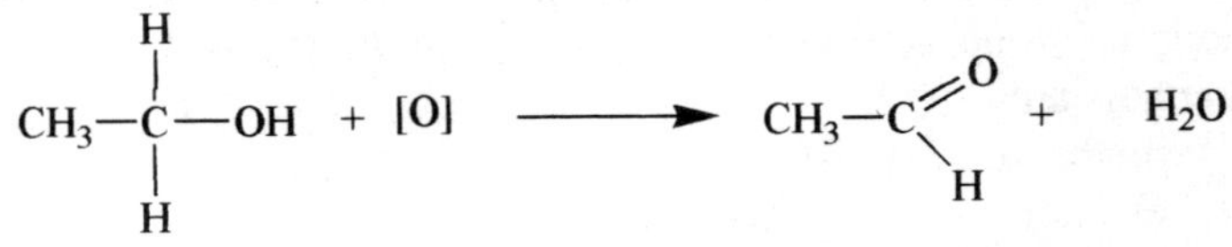

Ethanol Ethanal

An aldehyde still has one hydrogen atom attached to the carbonyl carbon so can be oxidised one step further to a carboxylic acid.

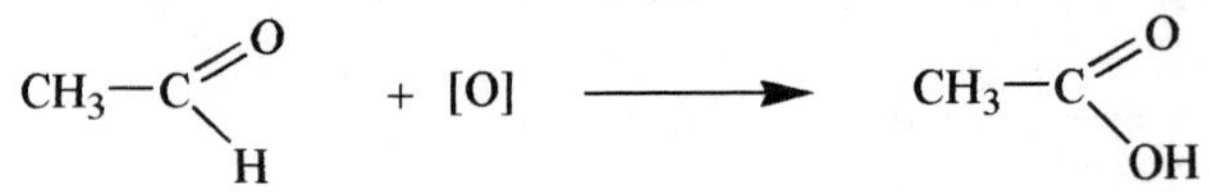

Ethanal Ethanoic acid

Alcoholic drinks such as wine that are left exposed to air go sour because the ethanol present is oxidised by bacteria to ethanoic acid. If the concentration of alcohol is above about 20%, this is too high for the bacteria to tolerate so the drink is not oxidised. This applies to all spirits and also to fortified wines such as sherry or port.

In practice, a primary alcohol such as ethanol is dripped into a warm mixture of acidified potassium dichromate(VI). The aldehyde ethanal is formed and immediately distils off thereby preventing further oxidation to ethanoic acid. This is because the boiling point of ethanal (23 °C) is much lower than that either of the original alcohol ethanol (78 °C) or of ethanoic acid (118 °C). Both the alcohol and the acid contain hydrogen bonding.

If oxidation of ethanol to ethanoic acid is required, the reagents must be refluxed together to prevent escape of the aldehyde before it can be oxidised further.

Secondary alcohols are oxidised to ketones. These have no hydrogens attached to the carbonyl carbon so cannot easily be oxidised further.

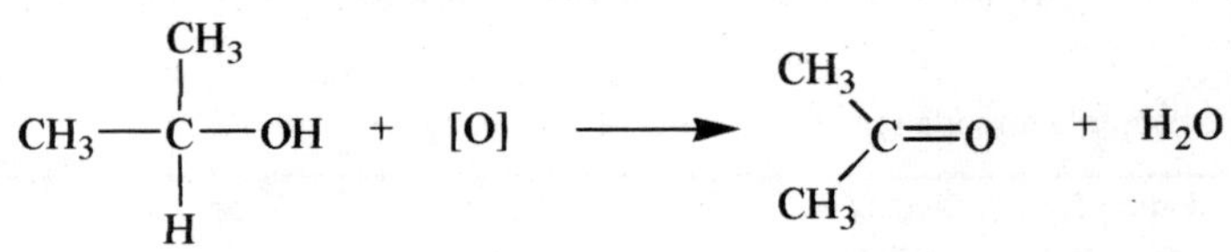

Propan-2-ol Propanone

When orange potassium dichromate(VI) acts as an oxidising agent, it is reduced to green chromium(III) ions Primary and secondary alcohols both turn acidified dichromate(VI) from orange to green when they are oxidised. This colour change can be used to distinguish tertiary alcohols from primary and secondary. Tertiary alcohols are not oxidised by acidified dichromate(VI) ions, so they have no effect on its colour which remains orange.

The formation of alkenes from alcohols

All alcohols can be dehydrated to alkenes when heated to 180 °C with concentrated sulphuric or concentrated phosphoric acid. The mechanism is an *elimination* and involves the formation a protonated alcohol which loses water to form a carbonium ion. This ion then loses a proton to produce an alkene. H^+ ions are used in the first step but released in the final step, i.e. the reaction is acid catalysed; e.g. the dehydration of propan-2-ol to propene,

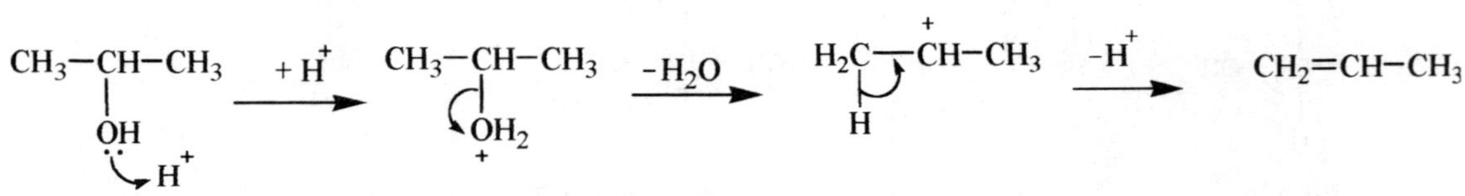

Similarly cyclohexanol forms cyclohexene and ethanol forms ethene.

Some alcohols may form more than one alkene on dehydration; e.g. butan-2-ol can form but-1-ene and but-2-ene but the latter is the major product.

3.2.8 Carbonyl compounds

The carbonyl compounds are aldehydes and ketones. Both sets of compounds have the general formula $C_nH_{2n}O$ and contain the carbonyl functional group.

Methanal, the first aldehyde, has two hydrogens attached to the carbonyl group. All other aldehydes have one hydrogen and one alkyl or aryl group. Ketones have two alkyl or aryl groups.

Aldehydes are formed by the oxidation of primary alcohols and are distilled away from the oxidising mixture before further oxidation to carboxylic acids can take place. Reduction of carboxylic acids, however, is not an effective way to produce aldehydes.

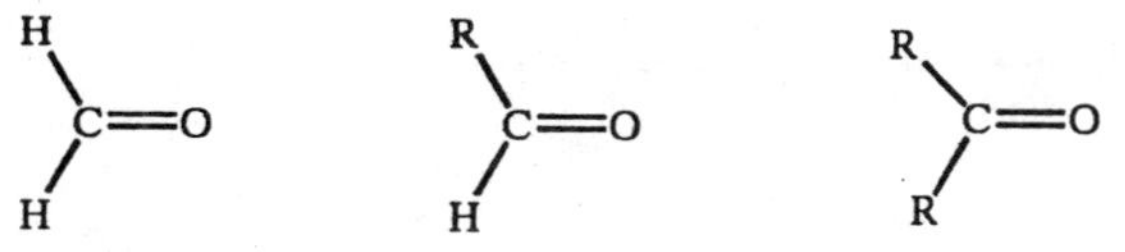

Methanal Aldehyde Ketone

The carbonyl group is planar, i.e. the carbon, the oxygen and the two atoms attached to the carbon all lie in a plane. Methanal is therefore a planar molecule.

Some examples of aldehydes and ketones are shown below:

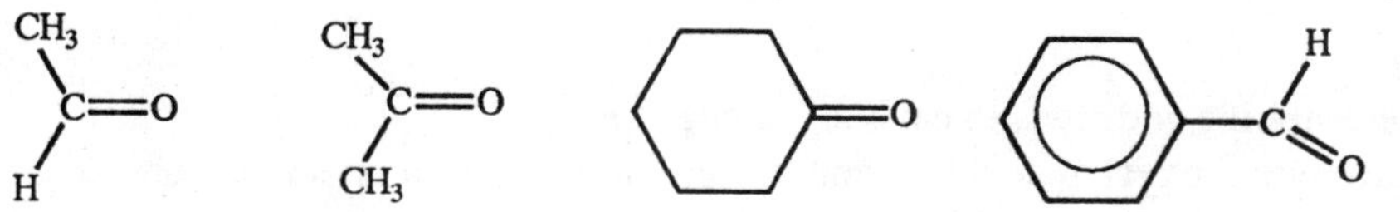

Ethanal Propanone Cyclohexanone Benzenecarbaldehyde *(benzaldehyde)*

Distinguishing between aldehydes and ketones

Many of the reactions of aldehydes and ketones are similar and are those of the carbonyl group. The effect of oxidising agents, however, is different; aldehydes are easily oxidised to carboxylic acids but ketones are not easily oxidised. Observing whether or not oxidation reactions occur can therefore be used to distinguish between them.

Although kėtones are not easily oxidised, powerful oxidising agents will react with them, causing carbon-carbon bonds to break and forming mixtures of carboxylic acids. Any distinguishing reaction therefore must use mild oxidising agents to ensure that this does not occur. The following are two examples of mild oxidising agents.

Tollen's reagent contains the complex ion $[Ag(NH_3)_2]^+$, and is prepared by adding an excess of aqueous ammonia to silver nitrate solution. Aldehydes reduce this ion and produce a silver mirror on the walls of a test tube; ketones do not form a silver mirror.

Fehling's solution contains a deep blue copper(II) complex ion. This is reduced by aldehydes but not ketones to form a red precipitate of copper(I) oxide, Cu_2O.

The oxidation of aldehydes in these reactions can be represented by the equation:

$$RCHO + [O] \rightarrow RCOOH$$

Reduction of carbonyl compounds

Aldehydes can be reduced to primary alcohols and ketones to secondary alcohols. This can be achieved in two ways.

(a) by hydrogenation.

This involves reacting the carbonyl compound with hydrogen in the presence of a nickel or platinum catalyst. The carbon-oxygen double bond is saturated in exactly the same way as carbon-carbon double bonds are saturated when alkenes are hydrogenated. A molecule which contains both carbon-oxygen and carbon-carbon double bonds will be completely saturated when catalytically hydrogenated. e.g.

$$CH_3COCH_2CH_3 + H_2 \rightarrow CH_3CHOHCH_2CH_3$$

Butanone Butan-2-ol

$$CH_2 = CHCHO + 2H_2 \rightarrow CH_3CH_2CH_2OH$$

Prop-2-enal Propan-1-ol

(b) by reaction with $NaBH_4$, sodium tetrahydridoborate(III) in methanol.

This reagent adds hydrogen via nucleophilic attack on the carbonyl group (see below). Acidification of the intermediate ion produces the alcohol. Since the electron cloud of an alkene will repel nucleophiles, $NaBH_4$ has no effect on alkenes and can be used for selective reduction of aldehydes and ketones, e.g. ethanal is reduced to ethanol

Equations showing [H] as the reductant are acceptable in this case, but they must still balance.

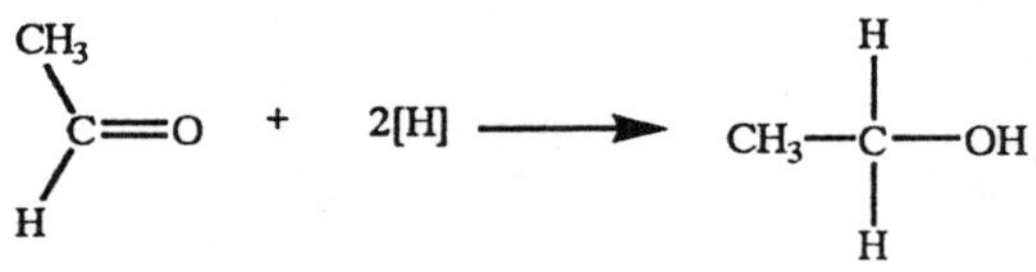

and propanone is reduced to propan-2-ol

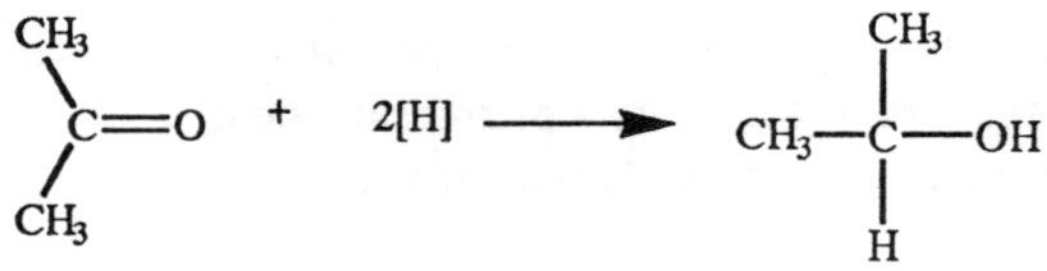

Nucleophilic additions to carbonyl compounds

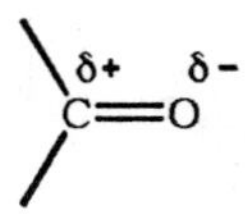

3.17

The carbon-oxygen double bond is an unsaturated link so is subject to addition reactions. Unlike the addition to alkenes, however, the electron cloud of the double bond is not evenly spread over the bond but is attracted by the electronegative oxygen. This produces an uneven distribution of electron density, i.e. a dipole, (see **3.17**).

The electron deficient (δ+) carbon atom is attractive to nucleophiles which bond to it in the first step of a nucleophilic addition reaction e.g. the formation of hydroxynitriles by the overall addition of HCN.

CH_3CHO + HCN → $CH_3CH(OH)CN$

ethanal — 2-hydroxypropanenitrile (a *cyanohydrin*)

The reaction is not usually carried out using the highly dangerous gas hydrogen cyanide, but by adding a carefully measured amount of dilute sulphuric acid to potassium cyanide to generate the gas in the reaction mixture.

The mechanism, outlined below, involves nucleophilic attack by the cyanide ion on the δ+ carbon followed by addition of a proton to the anion initially formed.

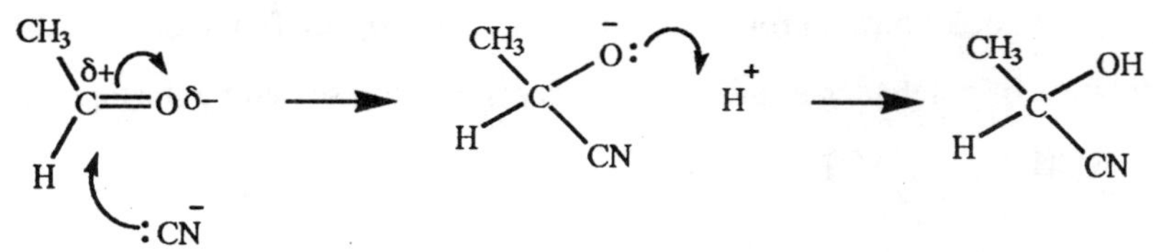

Note that all aldehydes (except methanal) and all unsymmetrical ketones (such as butanone) react with HCN to form compounds which contain an asymmetric carbon atom. However, the product obtained is an optically inactive racemic mixture. This is because attack by the cyanide nucleophile occurs with equal probability from either side of the planar carbonyl group (See 3.2.10)

The nitrile group (CN) can be hydrolysed to form a carboxylic acid group. This reaction can be used in the synthesis of hydroxycarboxylic acids such as 2-hydroxypropanoic (*lactic*) acid from aldehydes.

Naturally occurring lactic acid exists as one form, (e.g. that found in muscle tissue is the d-enantiomer). Lactic acid made in the laboratory, however, is a racemic mixture.

$CH_3CHO \xrightarrow{HCN} CH_3CH(OH)CN \xrightarrow{H^+(aq)} CH_3CH(OH)COOH$

Ethanal — 2-Hydroxypropanenitrile — 2-Hydroxypropanoic acid

3.2.9 Carboxylic acids and esters

Carboxylic acids contain the functional group -COOH with the structure **3.18.** Although the acid functional group, the carboxyl group, is made up of a *carb*onyl group (as in aldehydes and ketones) and a hydr*oxyl* group (as in alcohols), the two groups interact so that the properties of carboxylic acids are in the main different from both carbonyl compounds and alcohols.

The first three carboxylic acids are

- HCOOH — methanoic acid
- CH_3COOH — ethanoic acid
- CH_3CH_2COOH — propanoic acid

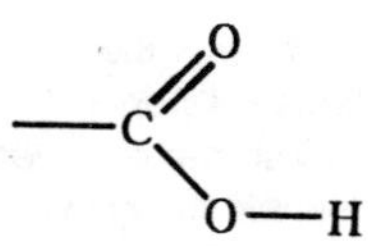

3.18

Acidity

Low molecular weight carboxylic acids are very soluble in water because the COOH group will hydrogen bond with water. The solubility is much lower, however, if the group attached is a long chain alkyl or aryl substituent when the influence of the carboxylic acid group on the overall physical properties is reduced.

Although the solubility may be high, the acids are only slightly dissociated in water, i.e. they are weak acids. The carbonyl group attracts electrons away from the alcohol group so the O-H bond is weakened and can break to release a proton and produce a carboxylate anion.

Carboxylate ion

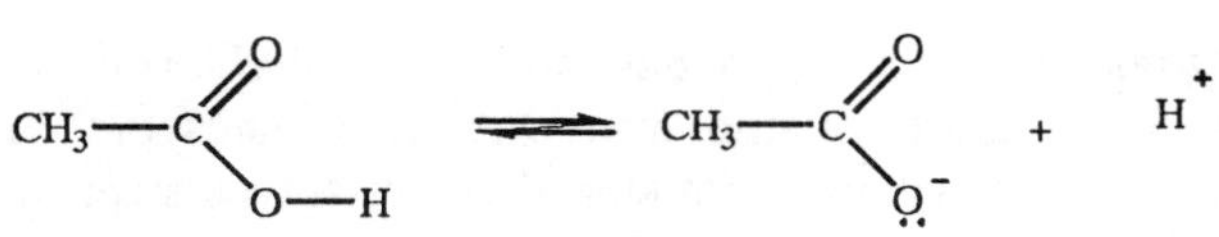

e.g. Ethanoic acid — Ethanoate ions

Unlike strong acids, this process does not go to completion, and in fact the amount of dissociation is quite small. The dissociation constant, K_a, for ethanoic acid is 1.8×10^{-5} mol dm^{-3}, which means that the acid is only about 0.3% ionised. The O-H bond in an alcohol by comparison does not break easily, hence alcohols are not acidic. The charge on the carboxylate anion is delocalised between the two oxygens. This means that the charge on each oxygen is effectively halved and the stabilised anion is less likely to regain a proton than expected.

$$Ka = \frac{[H^+][A^-]}{[HA]}$$

(see 4.3.1)

Carboxylic acids react as normal acids with metals, alkalis, or carbonates to form salts, although the reactions are less vigorous than with strong mineral acids.

When carboxylic acids react with sodium hydrogen carbonate, carbon dioxide is evolved. This reaction can be used as a test for the carboxylic acid group.

$$CH_3COOH + NaHCO_3 \rightarrow CH_3COONa + H_2O + CO_2$$

The salts formed are ionic and hence water soluble. An aromatic acid such as benzoic acid which is insoluble in water can be separated from other insoluble substances (which are not acidic) by the addition of dilute alkali. The acid reacts to form a water soluble salt which can be removed from the mixture. Addition of hydrochloric or other mineral acids will reform the carboxylic acid .

$$C_6H_5COOH(s) + NaOH(aq) \rightarrow C_6H_5COONa(aq) + H_2O(l)$$

$$C_6H_5COONa(aq) + HCl(aq) \rightarrow C_6H_5COOH(s) + NaCl(aq)$$

Esters

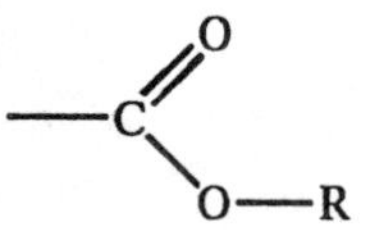

3.19

Ester formation involves the elimination of water. Isotopic labelling with ^{18}O shows that the OH group is lost from the acid and not the alcohol.

When making esters from carboxylic acids, carefully pour the equilibrium mixture formed into an excess of water. The remaining carboxylic acid dissolves but the ester is immiscible and floats on the water. The aroma of the ester is no longer contaminated with that of the acid.

Esters contain the functional group, COOR (**3.19**), where R can be an alkyl or an aryl group. Esters are formed by the reaction of carboxylic acids with alcohols in the presence of strong acid catalysts, e.g.

$$CH_3COOH + CH_3OH \rightleftharpoons CH_3COOCH_3 + H_2O$$

When pure ethanoic acid and methanol are mixed in the presence of concentrated sulphuric acid, the ester methyl ethanoate is formed as a volatile, sweet-smelling product.

Naming of esters

The ionic carboxylate group in salts of carboxylic acids is named by replacing the ending *-ic* from the name of the carboxylic acid with *-oate*. The acid part of an ester is similarly named, e.g. $CH_3CH_2COO^-$ is called propanoate

CH_3COO^- is called ethanoate

The alcohol part of the ester name is written first: so the complete name for

$CH_3CH_2COOCH_3$ is methyl propanoate

$HCOOCH_2CH_3$ is ethyl methanoate

$C_6H_5COOCH_2CH_3$ is ethyl benzenecarboxylate (*benzoate*)

Uses of esters

(a) as solvents

Esters have no free OH groups so cannot hydrogen bond as carboxylic acids or alcohols can. They are therefore much more volatile than carboxylic acids and are almost insoluble in water. Esters are polar however and will act as solvents for many polar organic compounds. Their relatively low boiling points allow them to be separated easily from the less volatile solutes. For example:

- Ethyl ethanoate (b.p. 77 °C) is commonly used as the solvent in glues such as polystyrene cement or in printing inks.
- Butyl ethanoate (b.p. 126.°C) is widely used as a solvent in the pharmaceutical industry, as a solvent for nitrocellulose, and as the solvent in many lacquers.

(b) as plasticisers

The loss of plasticiser over time, especially into fats, has called into question whether it is safe to use some types of cling film to wrap food. The acceptable maximum daily intake levels of DEHA, however, are so much higher than it is possible for a person to receive from normal use of cling film that such dangers are slight.

Although the forces between the chains in thermosoftening plastics are weak, the material is often not very soft or flexible because the polymer chains cannot easily move over each other. By incorporating into the polymer amounts of substances called plasticisers, which allow the chains some movement over each other, the flexibility of the material can be adjusted as required. The esters of benzene-1,2-dicarboxylic (*phthalic*) acid or of hexanedioic (*adipic*) acid are used for this purpose and can constitute up to 50% of some plastics such as PVC. Over a period of time, these additives escape from the plastic which becomes brittle and stiff with age.

Common plasticiser additives include DEHP [di-(2-ethylhexyl) phthalate] which is present in the PVC used to wrap food, or DEHA [di-(2-ethylhexyl) adipate] which is used in some cling films.

Cellulose ethanoate (*acetate*) is formed from cellulose by esterifying the OH links which cause hydrogen bonding between the cellulose chains. It is used for textiles such as artificial silks, e.g. rayon, and for photographic film.

(c) *food flavourings*

Many esters have sweet often fruity smells and are used as artificial fruit flavourings. Some of the common esters used in flavourings are shown in Table 3.8. Natural fruit flavours are extremely complex mixtures of several esters and carboxylic acids. Artificial flavours using only some of these compounds will inevitably only approximate to the real thing.

Table 3.8 Esters used as food flavourings

Name	Formula	Flavour
Pentyl ethanoate	$CH_3COOC_5H_{11}$	pear
2,2-Dimethylpropyl ethanoate	$CH_3COOC_5H_{11}$	banana
Octyl ethanoate	$CH_3COOC_8H_{17}$	orange
Ethyl butanoate	$C_3H_7COOC_2H_5$	rum
Pentyl pentanoate	$C_4H_9COOC_5H_{11}$	apple

Hydrolysis of esters

When esters are heated with alkali, hydrolysis occurs and an alcohol and a carboxylate salt are formed, e.g. ethyl ethanoate is hydrolysed in sodium hydroxide to produce ethanol and sodium ethanoate.

$$CH_3COOC_2H_5 + NaOH \rightarrow C_2H_5OH + CH_3COONa$$

This hydrolysis reaction is used widely with naturally occurring esters, such as oils and fats, to produce useful products including soaps and glycerol.

Most oils and fats are esters of propane-1,2,3-triol (*glycerol*) with three long chain carboxylic acids. These acids are often called fatty acids and the esters are called triglycerides.

Solid esters occur in animal fats; liquid esters are vegetable oils.

The most common fatty acids are:

- octadeca-9-enoic (*oleic*), an unsaturated acid which occurs in most fats and in olive oil,
- octadecanoic (*stearic*), a saturated acid which occurs in animal fats, and
- octadeca-9,12-dienoic (*linoleic*) acid, an unsaturated fat which is the principal acid in many vegetable oils such as soyabean and corn oil.

When these fats are boiled with sodium hydroxide, glycerol is formed and a mixture of the sodium salts of the three acids. These salts are soaps. e.g.

$CH_2OOC(CH_2)_{16}CH_3$
|
$CHOOC(CH_2)_{16}CH_3$ + 3NaOH ⟶ $CHOH$ + $3CH_3(CH_2)_{16}COONa$
|
$CH_2OOC(CH_2)_{16}CH_3$

(product: CH_2OH–$CHOH$–CH_2OH)

Propane-1,2,3-triol   Sodium octadecanoate (a soap)

Whereas the sodium salts of these long chain carboxylic acids are soluble in water, the calcium salts are not. Hence in hard water area, the calcium ions form unsightly scum with soap. Detergents, however, are salts of sulphonic acids, e.g. **3.20**. These form soluble calcium salts, so no scum is formed when a detergent is used.

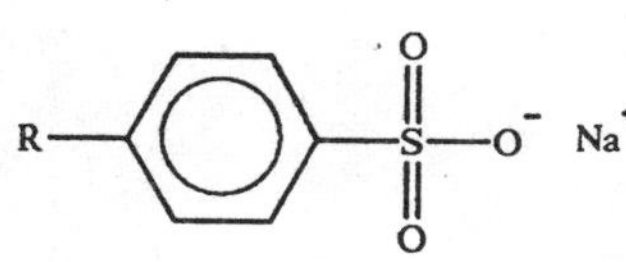

3.20

In practice, most soaps are mixtures of salts of long chain carboxylic acids since the fats and oils from which they are formed contain mixtures of these acids. Glycerol with its three OH bonds forms hydrogen bonds very easily and so has many applications which depend on its ability to attract water. It is used in the cosmetic industry, in foods, and in glues to prevent materials drying too soon. It is also an important component of wine, adding both to the sweetness and the viscosity.

3.2.10 Isomerism

Isomerism occurs where molecules with the same molecular formula have their atoms arranged in different ways. Isomerism is divided into two main types:

- *structural isomerism* and
- *stereoisomerism*

  but these are also subdivided.

Structural isomerism

Structural isomers are compounds with the same molecular formula but with different structures. Different structures can arise in three different ways.

(a) Chain isomerism

This occurs when there are two or more ways of arranging the carbon skeleton of a molecule, e.g. C_4H_{10} can be butane or 2-methylpropane.

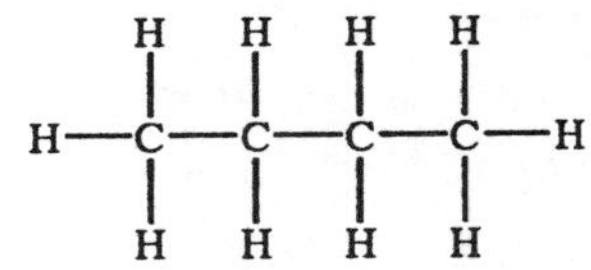

Butane

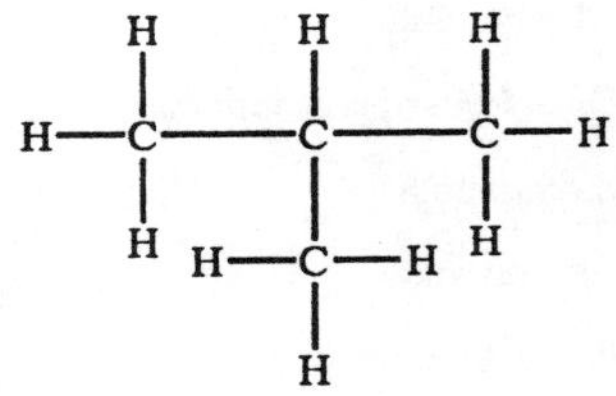

2-Methylpropane

The three isomers of C_5H_{12} are pentane, 2-methylbutane, and 2,2-dimethylpropane.

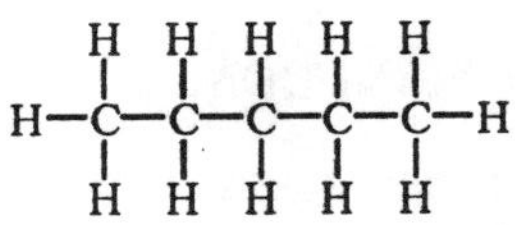

Pentane

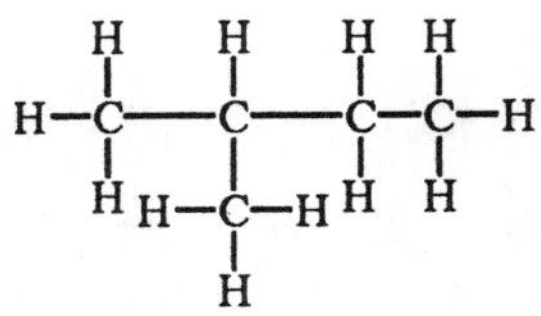

2-Methylbutane

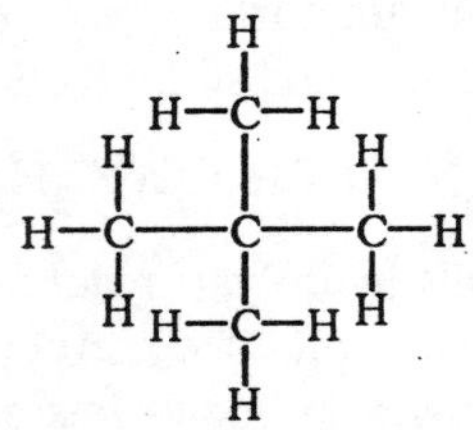

2,2-Dimethylpropane

These isomers have similar chemical properties but slightly different physical properties. Branched isomers have lower surface areas and so weaker van der Waals' forces and lower boiling points.

The number of structural isomers of alkanes rises steeply as the number of carbon atoms increases, see Table 3.9.

Table 3.9 The number of structural isomers of some alkanes

number of carbons	number of isomers
1	1
2	1
3	1
4	2
5	3
6	5
7	9
8	18
9	35
10	75
11	159
12	355
13	802
14	1,858
15	4,347
20	366,319
25	36,797,588
30	4,111,846,763
40	62,491,178,805,831

(b) Position isomerism

These isomers have the same carbon skeleton and the same functional group, but the functional group is joined in a different place, e.g.

$CH_3CH_2CH_2Br$	$CH_3CHBrCH_3$
1-Bromopropane	2-Bromopropane
$CH_2{=}CHCH_2CH_3$	$CH_3CH{=}CHCH_3$
But-1-ene	But-2-ene

These isomers have similar chemistry because they have the same functional group, but the different positions can cause some differences in properties.

(c) Functional group

These isomers have different functional groups so have different chemical and physical properties, e.g.

(i) aldehydes and ketones, e.g. C_3H_6O can be

CH_3CH_2CHO	or	CH_3COCH_3
Propanal		Propanone

(ii) carboxylic acids and esters, e.g. $C_3H_6O_2$ can be

CH_3CH_2COOH	CH_3COOCH_3	or	$HCOOCH_2CH_3$
Propanoic Acid	Methyl ethanoate		Ethyl methanoate

(iii) alcohols and ethers, e.g. C_2H_6O can be:

CH_3CH_2OH	or	CH_3OCH_3
Ethanol		Methoxymethane

Conditions for Reactions

Cracking	- 800°C (thermal)
	- 450°C + silica / alumina (catalytic
Chlorination of Methane	- UV light
Hydrogenation of Ethene	- 150°C, nickel
Hydration of Ethene	- 300 °C, 65 atmos., phosphoric acid
Nitration of Benzene	- conc. H_2SO_4, conc. HNO_3
Haloalkanes - substitution with OH^-	- warm, NaOH
- " " CN^-	- warm, $KCN_{(aq)}$
- " " ammonia	- warm, NH_3 (excess)
Oxidation of alcohol / aldehyde / methanoic acid	- potassium dichromate (VI)
Dehydration of alcohols	- 180° C, conc. H_2SO_4
Reduction of carbonyls - hydrogenation	- H_2, nickel
Addition of HCN to carbonyls	- KCN, HCl
Production of ester from acid & alcohol	- conc. H_2SO_4
Hydrolysis of esters	- heat with alkali (NaOH)

Stereoisomerism

Stereoisomers have the same structural formula but the bonds are arranged differently in space. The two types of stereoisomerism are *geometric* and *optical.*

(a) Geometric isomerism (*cis - trans*)

Because of the π electron clouds present above and below the plane of the bond, carbon-carbon double bonds in alkenes cannot rotate. If an alkene has 2 different groups on each end of the double bond *cis-trans* isomerism will result. *Cis* means that two groups are on the same side of the double bond and *trans* means they are on the opposite side, e.g. but-2-ene exists as two forms, identical except in the arrangement of the bonds in space.

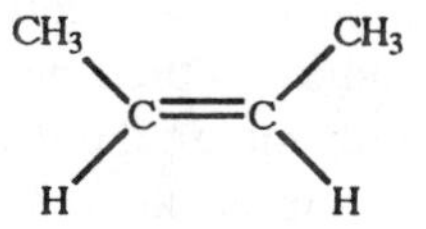

cis but-2-ene

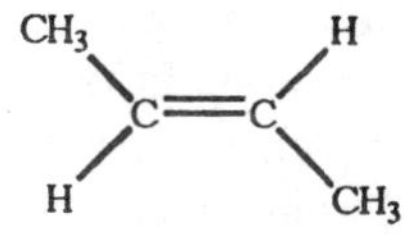

trans but-2-ene

Geometric isomers have different physical and chemical properties. *Cis*-isomers usually have slightly higher boiling points as they will have some polarity whereas *trans*-isomers are less polar. The b.p. of *cis*-but-2-ene is 4 °C whereas the b.p. of *trans*-but-2-ene is 1 °C. *Trans*-isomers however have higher melting points because they pack together better, e.g. the m.p. of *cis*-but-2-ene is -139 °C whereas the m.p. of *trans*-but-2-ene is -106 °C.

(b) Optical isomerism

If four different groups are attached to a carbon atom, the molecule has no centre, plane, or axis of symmetry. This means that it is different from its mirror image and not superimposable on it. The molecule is said to be *chiral* and to have an asymmetric carbon atom, e.g. 2-hydroxypropanenitrile exists in two forms which differ only in the way the bonds are arranged in space, that is they are stereoisomers.

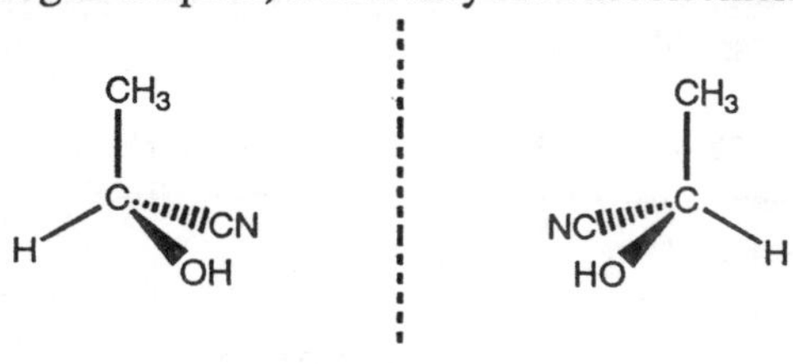

mirror

Optical activity was involved in the tragedy of the drug *thalidomide* in the 1960s. At this time many children were born without limbs to mothers who had taken the drug in the early months of pregnancy to reduce the effects of morning sickness. The drug as prescribed was a mixture of both isomers, one was an excellent sedative but its enantiomer had such awful side effects.

Molecules which possess an asymmetric carbon have one notable property. They rotate the plane of polarised light and are said to be optically active. Such optical isomers are also known as *enantiomers.*

If polarised light, i.e. light which is made up of waves vibrating in one plane only, is passed through a solution containing one of these enantiomers, the plane of the light is rotated either to the left [laevo or (-)] or to the right [dextro or (+)]. The other enantiomer, at the same concentration, will rotate the light equally in the opposite direction. A mixture of equal amounts of both enantiomers is optically inactive as the two effects cancel out. Such a solution is called a *racemic mixture* or a *racemate.*

Many naturally occurring molecules are optically active, in particular most amino acids, such as 2-aminopropanoic acid (*alanine*), (3.21) and sugars, such as glucose (3.9).

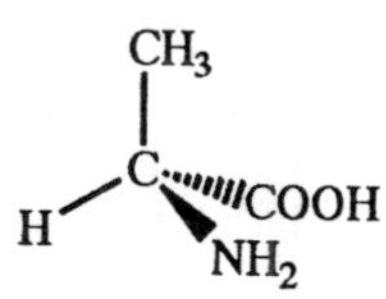

3.21

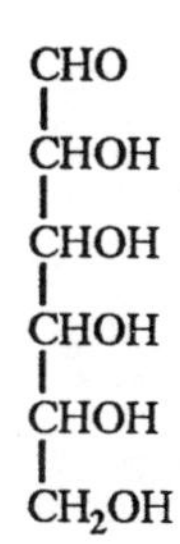

3.9

Enantiomers have identical physical properties and their chemical properties are the same except in reactions with other optically active substances. Enzymes are stereospecific and can distinguish between enantiomers; they will catalyse the reactions of one isomer but not the other.

2-Hydroxypropanenitrile can be prepared by the reaction of hydrogen cyanide with ethanal (see 3.2.8). Because the carbonyl group is planar, attack on the δ+ carbon in ethanal by the nucleophile, CN^-, is equally likely from above and below the plane so a racemic mixture of the two enantiomers is obtained. Hydrolysis of this product causes the cyanide group to be converted into a carboxylic acid group. The new product is a racemate of 2-hydroxypropanoic (lactic) acid. Naturally occurring lactic acid in muscles is just the (d-) or (+)-form but the lactic acid in sour milk is a racemic mixture.

3.2.11 Instrumental methods of analysis

Although traditional methods of analysis, gravimetric (by weighing) and volumetric (by titration), are still important, modern chemical analysis now uses the instrumental methods of infra-red spectroscopy, nuclear magnetic resonance spectroscopy and mass spectrometry. The chemist will often piece together information from all three techniques to be completely sure of the identity of an organic molecule.

Infra-red spectroscopy

The technique of i.r spectroscopy uses the natural frequency of vibration of particular bonds to identify the functional groups present in a molecule. The atoms in a molecule are in constant motion relative to each other because of the bending and stretching of bonds. When radiation across the full frequency range is passed through a substance, bonds absorb energy in the infra-red region corresponding to their natural frequency of vibration. This frequency depends on the bond strength and on the masses of the atoms bonded together. Strong bonds and low atomic masses vibrate at, and so absorb at, high frequencies while weak bonds and high masses absorb at low frequencies. The frequency of vibration for a particular bond, although not absolutely constant, does not change greatly from molecule to molecule. It is therefore possible to draw up a table of typical absorption frequencies.

Molecular vibrations typically occur in the range 1.2×10^{13} to 1.2×10^{14} Hz (s^{-1}). To avoid the need for such large numbers, absorptions are usually quoted in wavenumbers (the reciprocal of wavelength or the number of wavelengths in one cm) with unit cm^{-1}.

The infra-red spectrum is conveniently divided into four regions for purposes of structure interpretation, (see Table 3.10)

Infra-red absorptions occur in the frequency range 400 - 4000 cm^{-1}. This corresponds to an absorption of energy of between 4.8×10^3 and 4.8×10^4 J mol^{-1}. Note that this is absorption of joules of energy not kilojoules. Absorption of this many kilojoules of energy would break the bonds not merely cause them to stretch or bend.

Table 3.10 Regions of infra-red absorptions

Region /cm^{-1}	Absorptions
4000 - 2500	C—H, O—H, N—H
2500 - 2000	C≡C, C≡N
2000 - 1500	C = C, C = O, C = N
1500 - 400	C—C, C—O, C—N, C—X

The region below 1500 cm^{-1} is called the *fingerprint* region. In this region, spectra are complicated with many absorptions due to the large number of single bond vibrations. Molecules can be identified by comparing their spectra with those of known substances. Even if the absorptions by two different molecules in other regions of a spectrum are very similar, the fingerprint region is unique to each molecule so the two can be distinguished.

Table 3.11 shows some characteristic infra-red absorptions due to bond stretching in organic molecules. Each bond is shown absorbing over a range of wavelengths. Some variation in absorption will arise from the effect of adjacent groups on the bonds in question, e.g. the carbonyl group C=O absorbs in the region 1680 - 1750 cm^{-1}. A more detailed list of wavenumbers could show the differences between the C=O bond in aldehydes, ketones, carboxylic acids, and esters.

Interpretation of spectra

The spectra shown below are those of

Propanone	Fig. 3.15
Methyl ethanoate	Fig. 3.16
Ethanoic acid	Fig. 3.17

All three show very strong absorption in the region 1700 - 1750 cm^{-1} which confirms the presence of a carbonyl group.

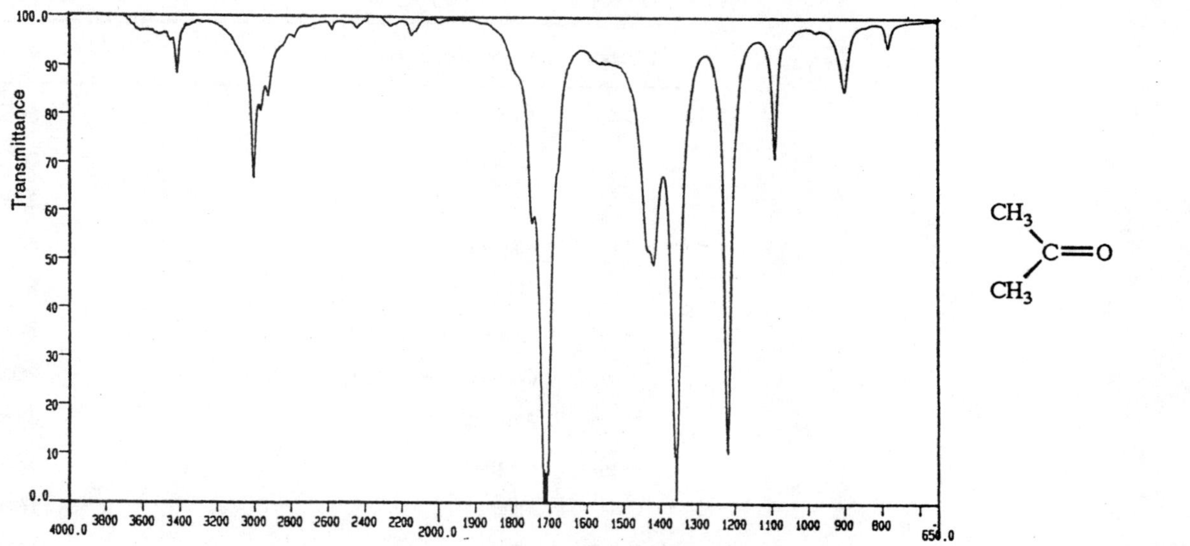

Fig. 3.15 Infra-red absorption spectrum of propanone.

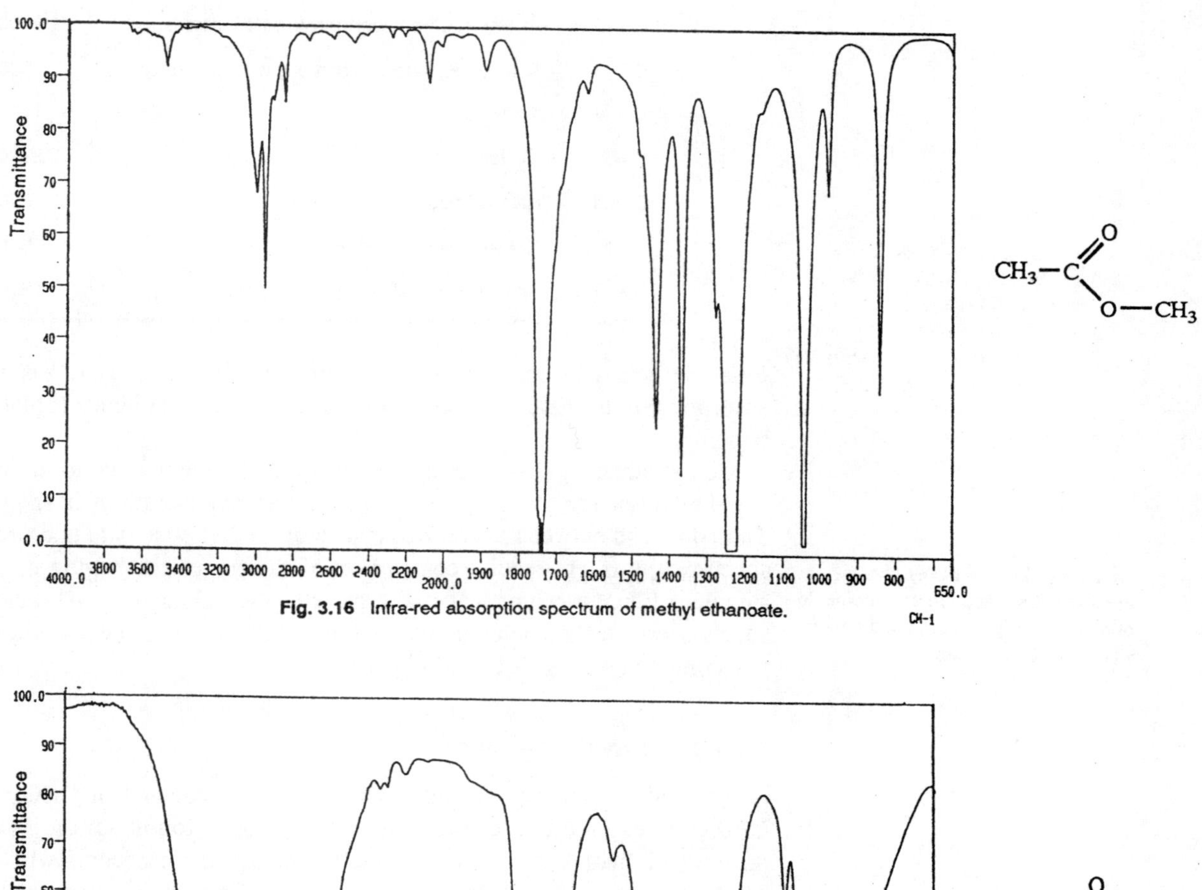

Fig. 3.16 Infra-red absorption spectrum of methyl ethanoate.

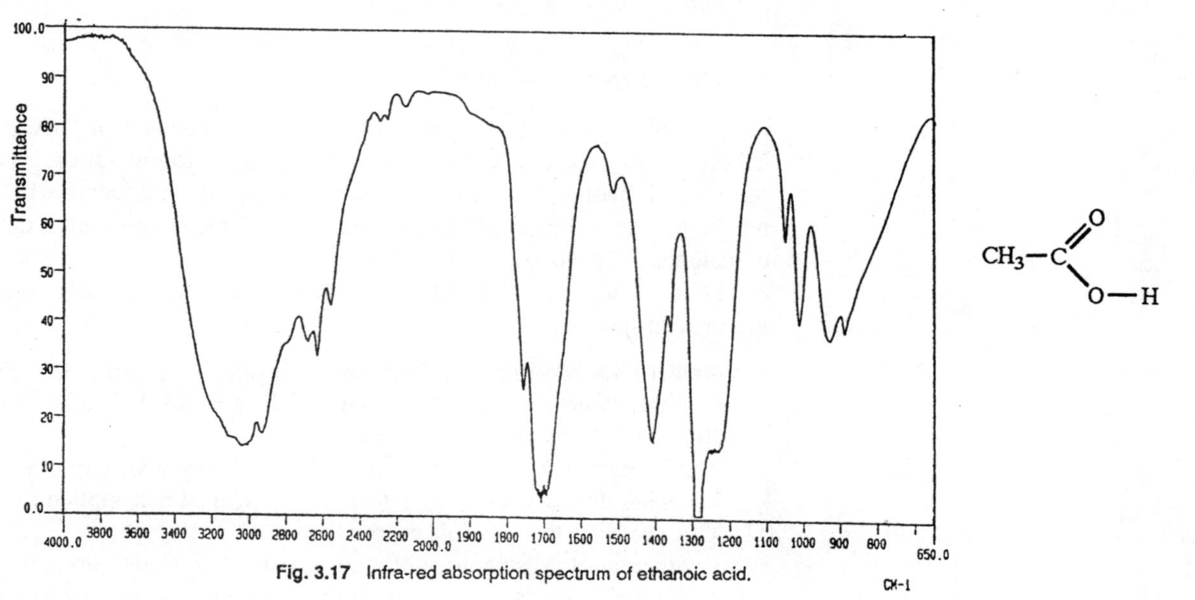

Fig. 3.17 Infra-red absorption spectrum of ethanoic acid.

Table 3.11 Characteristic infra-red absorptions due to bond stretching in organic molecules.

Bond	Types of compound	Range/cm^{-1}
C—H	Alkanes	2850 - 2960
	Alkenes	3010 - 3095
	Arenes	3250 - 3300
	Alkynes	3030 - 3080
	Aldehydes	2710 - 2730
O—H	Alcohol (H-bonded)	3230 - 3550
	Carboxylic acids (H-bonded)	2500 - 3000
N—H	Amines	3320 - 3560
C—C	Alkanes	750 - 1100
C = C	Alkenes	1620 - 1680
C ≡ C	Alkynes	2100 - 2250
C—C	Arenes	1500 - 1600
C—O	Alcohols, ethers, carboxylic acids, esters	1000 - 1300
C = O	Aldehydes, ketones, carboxylic acids, esters	1680 - 1750
C—N	Amines	1180 - 1360
C ≡ N	Nitriles	2210 - 2260
C—Cl	Haloalkanes	600 - 800
C—Br	Haloalkanes	500 - 600
N—O	Aryl nitro derivative	1330 - 1550

Ethanoic acid can be distinguished from the other two as it has the strong, broad absorption in the 3000 cm^{-1} region characteristic of O-H bonds (broad due to hydrogen bonding).

Methyl ethanoate has a strong absorption at 1280 cm^{-1} due to the C-O bond but this could be missed in the midst of a large number of absorptions in the fingerprint region. To distinguish between unknown samples of methyl ethanoate and propanone using i.r. spectroscopy might require comparison of the fingerprint region of spectra of known samples of the two compounds with those of the unknowns. Alternatively, a different spectroscopic technique might be used in addition to i.r., (see the n.m.r. spectra of these two compounds, Fig. 3.18 and Fig. 3.19).

On its own i.r. can rarely give a complete identification of a molecule and is normally used in conjunction with other techniques.

Nuclear magnetic resonance

A more detailed theory of n.m.r. spectroscopy is covered in CH06. Candidates for CH03 are required to use spectra to obtain information about the relative number and position of hydrogen atoms in a molecule, but these spectra will either be at low resolution (i.e. without spin-spin coupling) or of molecules where there are no protons on neighbouring atoms.

The following is a brief outline of the theory of n.m.r. to assist understanding of this use of such spectra.

- Nuclei with odd mass numbers have a property of spin. We shall consider only spin due to protons, ^{1}H. Note that ^{2}H (deuterium), ^{12}C, and ^{16}O nuclei have zero spin.
- This nuclear spin induces weak magnetic fields which interact with an external magnetic field and can align either with or against this applied field.
- This produces two possible energy levels.
- Irradiation of a sample with the correct frequency produces resonance when absorption of energy causes transitions between these energy levels.

- The environment of the proton, i.e. the bonds adjacent, will affect the electron density around it and modify both the induced magnetic field and hence the frequency of absorption. This difference is very small, only a few parts per million (ppm).
- Spectra are usually measured by keeping the radiofrequency constant and varying the strength of the applied magnetic field.
- The scale used is not expressed in frequency units, but is known as the chemical shift. This is independent both of the magnetic field used and the frequency range of the instrument.
- Chemical shifts are given relative to a standard, tetramethylsilane $(CH_3)_4Si$ (TMS), which gives a reference peak with a shift of zero.
- Chemical shifts for hydrogen (δH) are expressed as parts per million and have values between 0 and 12.
- Tables of chemical shifts can be used to identify specific types of proton.

N.m.r. spectra give the following pieces of information about chemical structure:

- the *number of absorptions* indicates how many types of non-equivalent protons are present,
- the *positions of the absorptions* gives clues to the environment of each kind of proton,
- the *intensities of the absorptions*, as shown by the area of each peak, indicate how many equivalent protons are associated with each absorption peak. This is sometimes given on a spectrum as an *integration trace*; i.e. the spectrometer measures the areas of the peaks and shows this as a curve. The relative heights of the integration curve at each peak can be used to discover the relative numbers of protons associated with the peak.

Spin-spin coupling will give information about neighbouring protons, (see 6.4.3).

Interpretation of spectra

The spectra shown below are those of

Propanone	Fig. 3.18
Methyl ethanoate	Fig. 3.19
Ethanol	Fig. 3.20

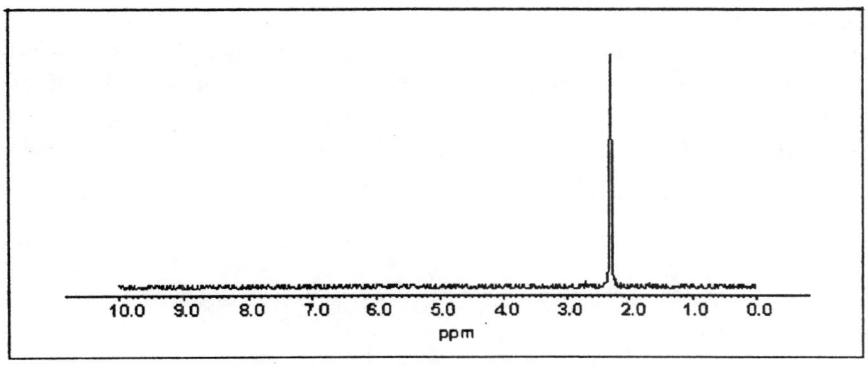

Fig. 3.18 N.m.r. spectrum of propanone.

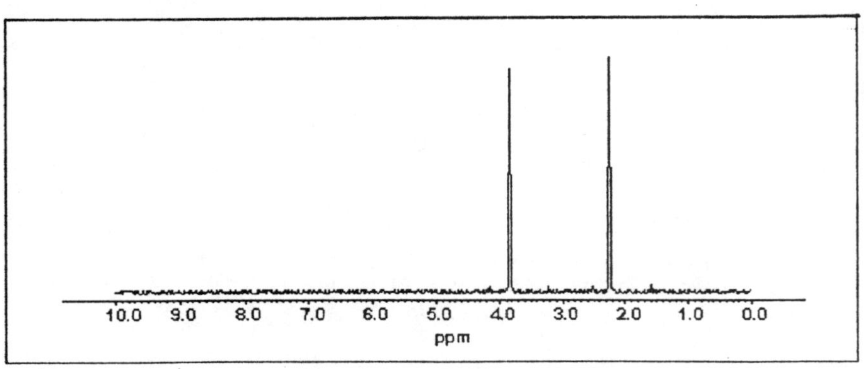

Fig. 3.19 N.m.r. spectrum of methyl ethanoate.

The peak at 3.8 ppm corresponds to the protons of the OCH_3 group. These are deshielded by the electronegative oxygen so are at lower field than the protons in the CH_3CO part of the molecule.

For the high resolution n.m.r. spectrum of ethanol showing splitting of the peaks see 6.4.3.

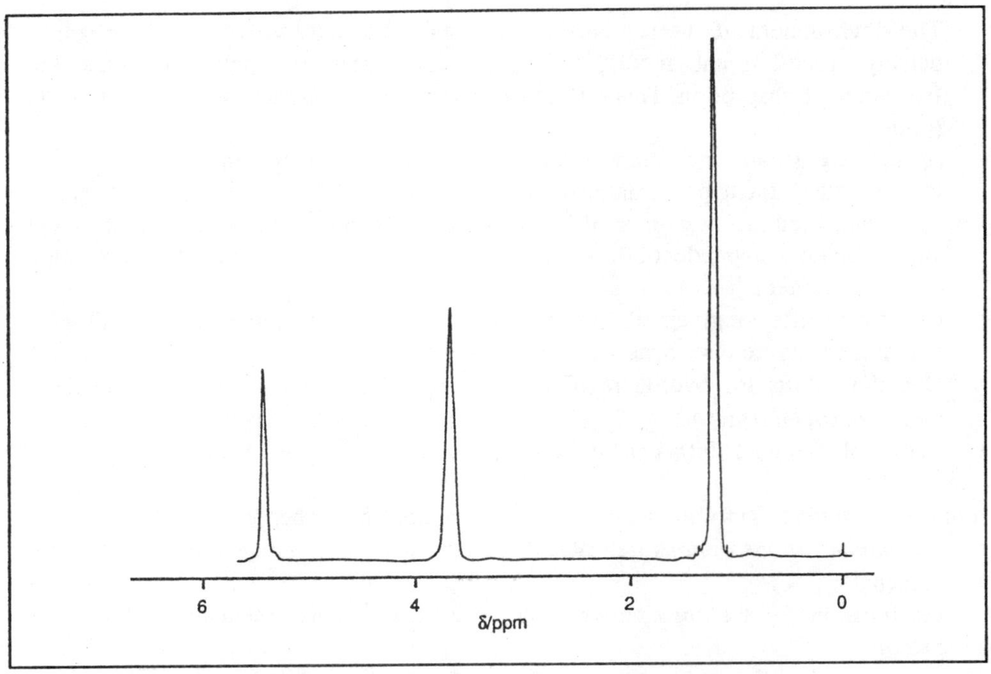

Fig.3.20 Low resolution n.m.r. spectrum of ethanol

All six hydrogens in propanone are equivalent. The n.m.r. spectrum, (Fig. 3.18), therefore shows only one peak.
Methyl ethanoate also contains six protons but these are present as two separate methyl groups. The n.m.r. spectrum, (Fig. 3.19), therefore has two peaks of equal height.
Ethanol has six protons in three different environments, CH_3 ($\delta = 1.22$ ppm), CH_2 ($\delta = 3.70$ ppm.), and OH ($\delta = 5.74$ ppm). Fig. 3.20, the low resolution n.m.r. spectrum of ethanol, shows three peaks with the areas in the expected ratio of 3:2:1. For discussion of the high resolution n.m.r. spectrum of ethanol see 6.4.3).

Mass spectrometry

Relative molecular mass

If the molecular mass is odd there is probably an odd number of nitrogens present.

When a sample of an organic compound is introduced to a mass spectrometer, provided that the molecule is not completely fragmented, the peak at the maximum value of m/z corresponds to the molecular ion, M^+. The value of m/z for this ion is equal to the relative molecular mass, M_r, e.g. nitrobenzene, $C_6H_5NO_2$, with $M_r = 123$ (see Fig 3.21).

Interpretation of the fragmentation patterns in mass spectra is not required in CH03, (see 6.4.1).

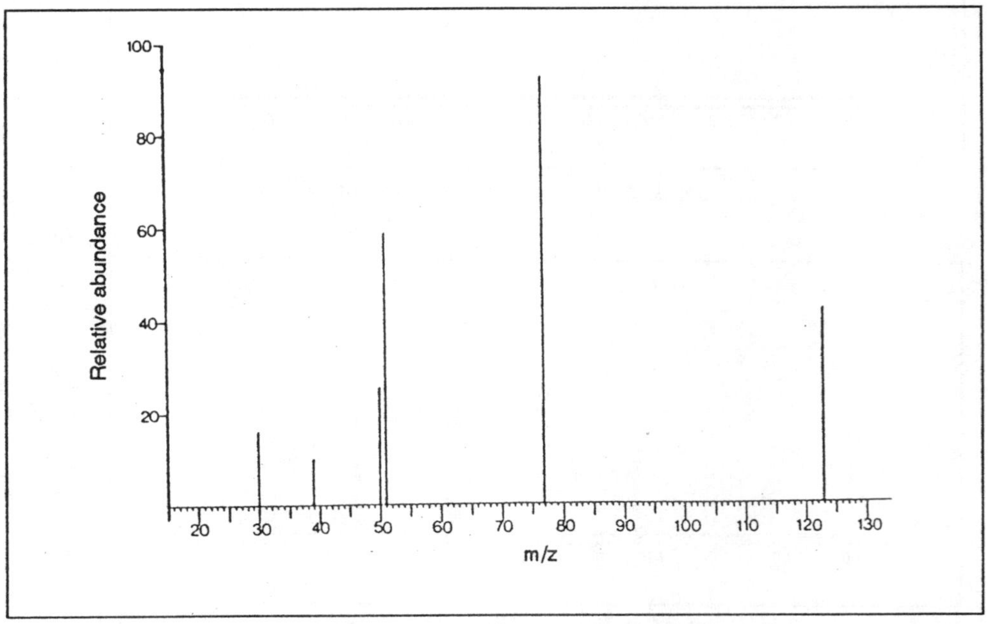

Fig. 3.21 Mass spectrum of nitrobenzene

Isotopes

If a molecule contains elements where isotopes are present, more than one molecular ion peak will be seen. Compounds containing chlorine with isotopes ^{35}Cl and ^{37}Cl with relative abundances 3 : 1, will have two molecular ion peaks two mass units apart and with relative intensities 3 : 1. Similarly compounds containing bromine, which has isotopes ^{79}Br and ^{81}Br with relative abundances 1 : 1, have two molecular ion peaks of equal intensity, e.g. 1-bromopropane, $CH_3CH_2CH_2Br$, has two molecular ion peaks at m/z = 122 and 124, (see Fig. 3.22).

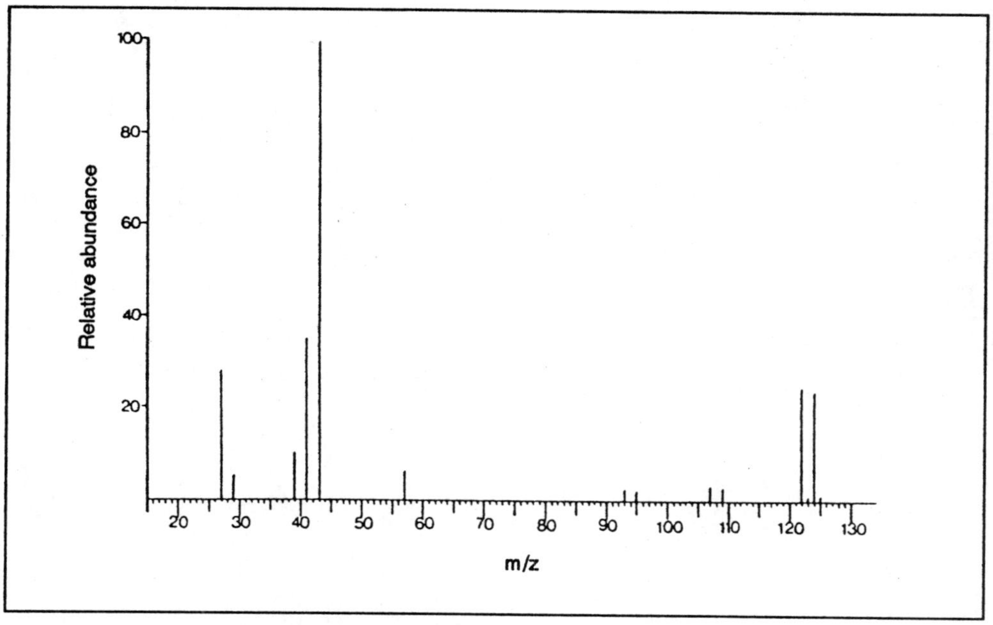

Fig 3.22. Mass spectrum of 1-bromopropane.

M+1 peaks occur due to the presence of ^{13}C. The relative abundance of this isotope is only small, 1.1% of ^{12}C, but the relative heights of the M and the M+1 peaks will show the number of carbon atoms present, e.g. if the ratio of heights of M to M+1 is 100 : 8.8, there are 8 carbon atoms in the molecule.

A module test, model answers for Section A, and an outline scheme for Section B are reproduced on the following pages.

The answers given are not necessarily the only acceptable ones for which credit would be given in an examination.

GCE

Northern Examinations and Assessment Board

NEAB

General Certificate of Education

Chemistry Advanced Supplementary
Chemistry Advanced
Kinetics and Organic Chemistry (CH3)
Module Test
Sections A and B

Tuesday 28 February 1995 9.30am – 11.00am

Centre name	
Centre number	Candidate number
Surname	
Other names	

In addition to this paper you will need a Periodic Table.
Questions for Section B which are included herein as a loose insert.

Instructions to candidates
- Write your name and other details in the spaces provided above.
- **Answer all the questions in this paper.**
  Write all your answers to both Sections A and B in this combined question paper/answer book.

Information for candidates
- **The total time for this paper is 1½ hours.**
- **You are recommended to spend 30 minutes on Section B.**
- The following data may be required.
  Gas constant $R = 8.31\ J\ mol^{-1}\ K^{-1}$.
- This paper carries 13⅔ per cent of the total marks for A-level. For the AS syllabus this paper carries 27⅓ per cent of the total mark.
- The allocation of marks to individual questions is given in the right-hand margin of the question paper.
- Candidates are reminded of the need for good English and clear presentation.

For examiner's use	
1	
2	
3	
4	
5	
6	
7	
Total	

Section A

Answer **all** the questions in the spaces provided.

1 Ethanal dimerises in dilute alkaline conditions to form compound **A** according to the equation:

$$2CH_3CHO \rightarrow \underset{\mathbf{A}}{CH_3CH(OH)CH_2CHO}$$

The following data were obtained in a study of the rate of the reaction.

$[CH_3CHO]$/mol dm^{-3}	$[OH^-]$/mol dm^{-3}	Initial rate of reaction (relative values)
0.10	0.015	1
0.20	0.015	2
0.40	0.030	8

(a) (i) Deduce the order of reaction with respect to ethanal.

....

(ii) Deduce the order of reaction with respect to hydroxide ions.

....

(iii) Hence write an overall rate equation.

....

(iv) Calculate the relative value of the initial rate of reaction when the concentration of ethanal is 0.30 mol dm^{-3} and the concentration of hydroxide is 0.030 mol dm^{-3}.

.... *(4)*

(b) Give the IUPAC (systematic) name for compound **A**.

.... *(1)*

For examiner's use only

(c) In **each** case, draw the structure of the organic product of the reaction of compound **A** with:

(i) an excess of acidified potassium dichromate(VI)

(ii) sodium tetrahydridoborate(III) ($NaBH_4$)

(3)

(d) What colour change would you see in the reaction taking place in (c)(i)?

.... *(2)*

(e) The dimerisation of ethanal produces compound **A** as a mixture of two isomers. Name the type of isomerism involved and name the structural feature in **A** which gives rise to it. Describe how the two isomers could be distinguished.

Type of isomerism ....

Structural feature in A ....

....

Method used to distinguish between isomers ....

....

.... *(4)*

(14)

Turn over ▶

For examiner's use only

2 A gas oil fraction from the distillation of crude oil contains hydrocarbons in the C_{15} to C_{19} range. These hydrocarbons can be cracked by strong heating.

(a) Explain why molecules of this size are chosen for cracking.

....

.... *(1)*

(b) Name **two** types of compound produced by cracking and give a different use for each.

Type 1 *Name* ....

Use ....

Type 2 *Name* ....

Use .... *(4)*

(c) Write the molecular formula for the alkane with 19 carbon atoms.

.... *(1)*

(d) Name the type of reaction involved in cracking.

.... *(1)*

(e) Write an equation for one possible cracking reaction of the alkane $C_{16}H_{34}$ when the products include ethene and propene in the molar ratio 2:1 and only one other compound.

....

.... *(2)*

(f) Write an equation for the formation of ethene from ethanol and give any necessary conditions for the reaction to be carried out in the laboratory.

Equation ....

Conditions .... (3)

(12)

For examiner's use only

3 When irradiated with ultraviolet light, methane reacts with chlorine to form a mixture containing several organic products.

(a) Name the type of mechanism involved.

.... *(1)*

(b) Explain why ultraviolet light is needed.

....

.... *(2)*

(c) Write an equation to show the formation of chloromethane from chlorine and methane.

.... *(1)*

(d) Another product has a relative molecular mass of 85. Identify this product and write that part of the mechanism which shows its formation from chloromethane.

Product with M_r 85 ....

Mechanism ....

.... *(3)*

(e) Explain how a small amount of ethane is formed in the process and name the mechanistic step which leads to its formation.

Explanation ....

....

Name of mechanistic step .... *(2)*

(f) Give the major product formed when methane reacts with a large excess of chlorine.

.... *(1)*

(10)

For examiner's use only

4 (a) Explain what is meant by the term *nucleophilic substitution*.

....

.... (2)

(b) Explain why l-bromopropane reacts with nucleophiles but propane itself does not.

....

....

.... (2)

(c) Write an equation and a mechanism for the reaction of l-bromopropane with an excess of ammonia.

Equation ....

Mechanism

(4)

(d) Give the starting materials and state the conditions for the preparation of CH_3CH_2CN by nucleophilic substitution.

Starting materials ....

....

Conditions .... (3)

(11)

For examiner's use only

5

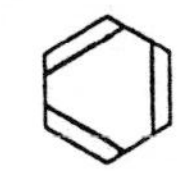

A

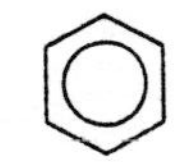

B

Benzene is sometimes written as structure **A** and sometimes as structure **B**.

(a) What is the significance of the circle in structure **B**?

....

.... (1)

(b) Structure **A** would suggest that benzene would react in the same way as an alkene such as cyclohexene. Give one reaction, other than combustion, that both benzene and cyclohexene will undergo. Write a balanced equation and give any necessary conditions for your example with cyclohexene.

Reaction ....

Equation for cyclohexene reaction

....

Conditions .... (3)

(c) (i) Choose a reaction that benzene will undergo but cyclohexene will not. For your reaction, write an equation, give the necessary reagents and name the type of mechanism.

Equation ....

Reagents ....

Name of mechanism .... (4)

(ii) Choose a reaction that cyclohexene will undergo but benzene will not. For your reaction, write an equation and name and outline the mechanism.

Equation ....

Name of mechanism ....

Mechanism

(5)

(13)

For examiner's use only

....

....

....

GCE

Northern Examinations and Assessment Board

NEAB

General Certificate of Education

Chemistry Advanced Supplementary
Chemistry Advanced
Kinetics and Organic Chemistry (CH3)

Module Test

Section B

In addition to this paper you will need
- a Periodic Table
- a combined question paper/answer book for Sections A and B.

Instructions to candidates
- Answer both the questions in Section B.
- Your answers should be written on pages 8-12 of the combined question paper/answer book.

Information for candidates
- You are advised to spend about 30 minutes on this section.
- The allocation of marks to individual questions is given in the right-hand margin of the question paper.
- You are reminded of the need for good English and clear presentation.

Insert to 6990

Section B

You are recommended to spend 30 minutes on this section.
Answer **both** questions on pages 8 to 12 of the combined question paper/answer book.

For examiner's use only

6 An ester **A** of molecular formula $C_4H_8O_2$ was hydrolysed to form a carboxylic acid **B** and an alcohol **C**.

(a) The structures of the four esters of molecular formula $C_4H_8O_2$ are shown below.

I	II	III	IV
$CH_3CH_2COOCH_3$	$CH_3COOCH_2CH_3$	$HCOOCH_2CH_2CH_3$	$HCOOCH(CH_3)_2$

For **each** structure predict the number of peaks in its low resolution n.m.r. spectrum corresponding to the different types of hydrogen and also the number of each different type of hydrogen. *(8)*

(b) The low resolution n.m.r. spectra of **A** and **B** are shown below with the number of hydrogens for each peak indicated. Use these spectra to decide which of the four esters is the correct one for **A** and explain your answer. *(3)*

Ester **A**

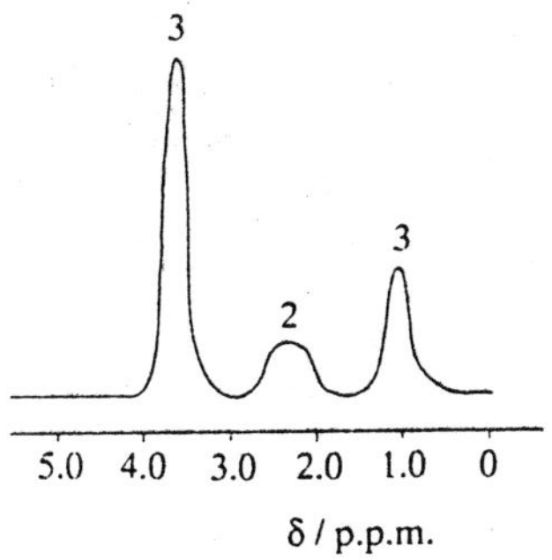

Acid **B**

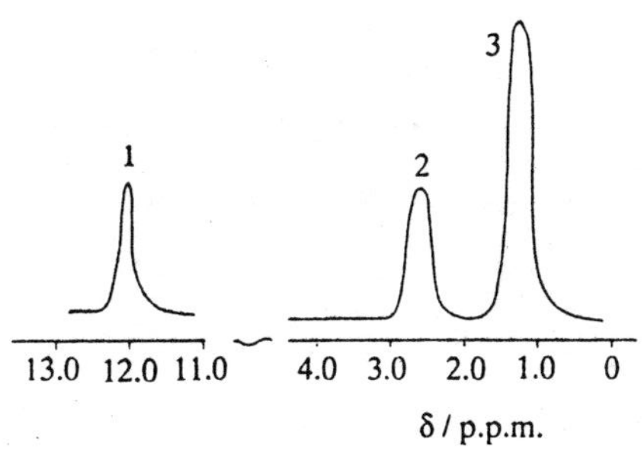

(c) The i.r. spectra 1-3 opposite are those of compounds **A**, **B** and **C** but not necessarily in that order. Use the table of i.r. absorption data to decide which spectrum corresponds to which compound and explain your answer. *(6)*

Table of i.r. absorption data

Bond	wavenumber / cm^{-1}
C – H	2840 – 3300
C – C	750 – 1100
C = C	1610 – 1680
C = O	1680 – 1750
C – O	1000 – 1300
O – H	3230 – 3550

For examiner's use only

Spectrum 1

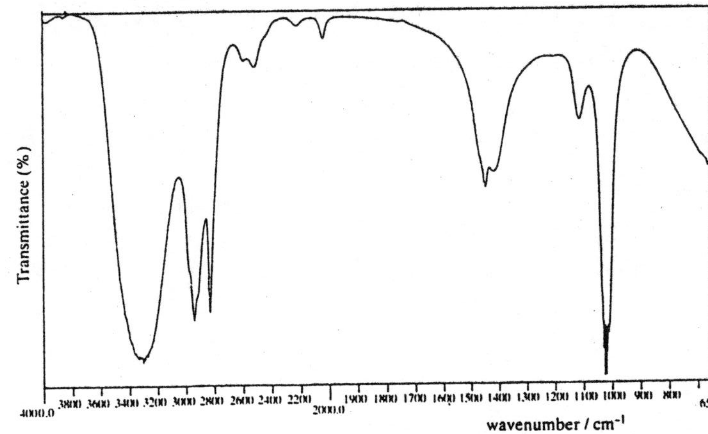

Spectrum 2

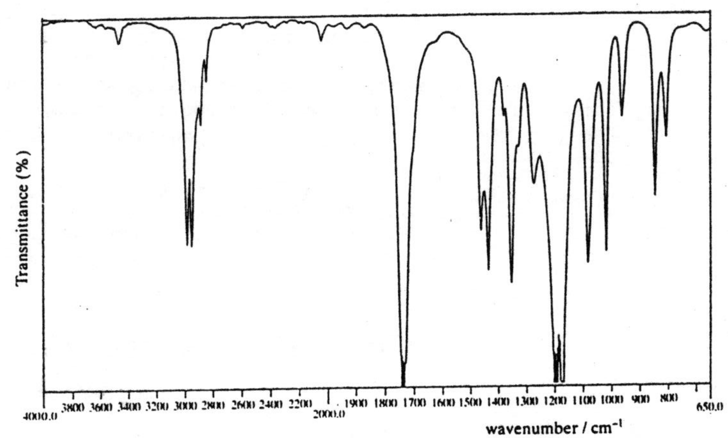

Spectrum 3

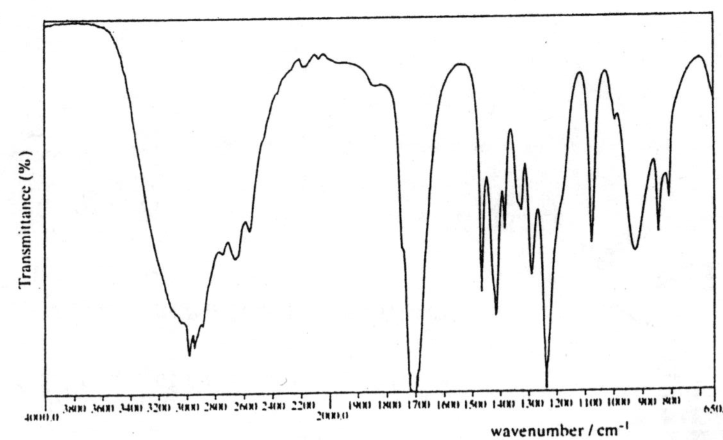

(17)

Turn over ▶

For examiner's use only

7 (a) (i) On the same axes draw Maxwell-Boltzmann distribution curves of molecular energies for a sample of gas at two different temperatures. Label the axes.

(ii) Use your answer in (a)(i) to explain why an increase in temperature increases the rate of a reaction. *(8)*

(b) The rate of a gas phase reaction varies with time as shown below. Explain the shape of the curve in terms of the behaviour of the molecules. *(5)*

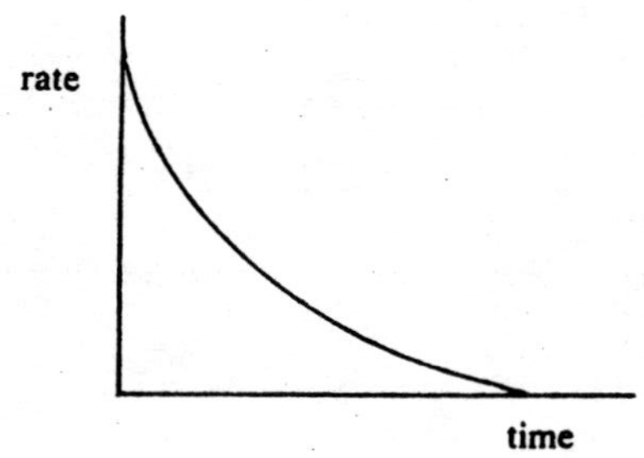

(13)

For examiner's use only

For examiner's use only

For examiner's use only

Model answers to Section A

&

outline scheme for Section B

Mark Scheme

GCE 1995

SPRING TESTS

Northern Examinations and Assessment Board

NEAB

Chemistry CH3 (Kinetics and Organic Chemistry)

- Each mark scheme is initially prepared by the relevant Principal Examiner. It is discussed and amended at a standardising meeting before examiners begin their marking.
- The standardising meeting is held to ensure that the scheme covers candidates' responses to questions and that every examiner understands it and applies it in the same way.
- This published mark scheme includes any amendments made and additional alternative answers included at the standardising meeting.
- It must be stressed that a mark scheme is a working document. It is not exhaustive; valid alternative answers and approaches not covered by the scheme will always be credited. Examiners refer to the Principal Examiner for advice about unusual answers which have not been included in the scheme.

The Northern Examinations and Assessment Board (NEAB) incorporates the Joint Matriculation Board (JMB) and the Northern Examining Association (NEA)

For examiner's use only

Section A

Answer **all** the questions in the spaces provided.

1 Ethanal dimerises in dilute alkaline conditions to form compound **A** according to the equation:

$$2CH_3CHO \rightarrow \underset{\textbf{A}}{CH_3CH(OH)CH_2CHO}$$

The following data were obtained in a study of the rate of the reaction.

$[CH_3CHO]$/mol dm^{-3}	$[OH^-]$/mol dm^{-3}	Initial rate of reaction (relative values)
0.10	0.015	1
0.20	0.015	2
0.40	0.030	8

(a) (i) Deduce the order of reaction with respect to ethanal.

1 (1)

(ii) Deduce the order of reaction with respect to hydroxide ions.

1 (1)

(iii) Hence write an overall rate equation.

rate = k $[CH_3CHO][OH^-]$ (1)

(iv) Calculate the relative value of the initial rate of reaction when the concentration of ethanal is 0.30 mol dm^{-3} and the concentration of hydroxide is 0.030 mol dm^{-3}.

×3 ×2 = 6 (1)

(4)

(b) Give the IUPAC (systematic) name for compound **A**.

3-hydroxybutanal (1)

(1)

For examiner's use only

(c) **In each case, draw the structure of the organic product of the reaction of compound A with:**

(i) an excess of acidified potassium dichromate(VI)

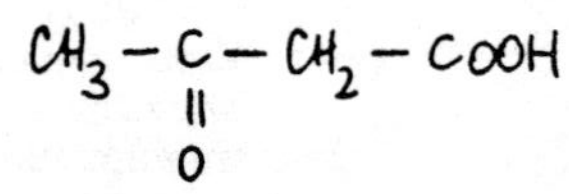

ketone (1)

acid (1)

(ii) sodium tetrahydridoborate(III) ($NaBH_4$)

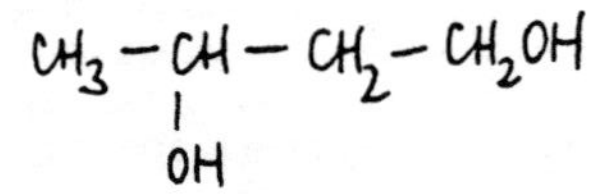

(1)

(3)

(d) What colour change would you see in the reaction taking place in (c)(i)?

orange (1) → green (1)

(2)

(e) The dimerisation of ethanal produces compound **A** as a mixture of two isomers. Name the type of isomerism involved and name the structural feature in **A** which gives rise to it. Describe how the two isomers could be distinguished.

Type of isomerism optical (1)

Structural feature in A asymmetric carbon (1)

Method used to distinguish between isomers

polarised light (1)

plane rotated in opposite directions (1)

(4)

(14)

Turn over ▶

For examiner's use only

2 A gas oil fraction from the distillation of crude oil contains hydrocarbons in the C_{15} to C_{19} range. These hydrocarbons can be cracked by strong heating.

(a) Explain why molecules of this size are chosen for cracking.

demand for C_8 > supply
or " " C_{15} < " } (1) — *(1)*

(b) Name **two** types of compound produced by cracking and give a different use for each.

Type 1 Name alkane (1)

Use petrol (1)

Type 2 Name alkene (1)

Use making polymers (1) — *(4)*

(c) Write the molecular formula for the alkane with 19 carbon atoms.

$C_{19}H_{40}$ (1) — *(1)*

(d) Name the type of reaction involved in cracking.

radical or homolytic fission (1) — *(1)*

(e) Write an equation for one possible cracking reaction of the alkane $C_{16}H_{34}$ when the products include ethene and propene in the molar ratio 2:1 and only one other compound.

$C_{16}H_{34} \rightarrow 2C_2H_4 + C_3H_6 + C_9H_{20}$

or $C_{16}H_{34} \rightarrow 4C_2H_4 + 2C_3H_6 + C_2H_6$ (2) — *(2)*

(f) Write an equation for the formation of ethene from ethanol and give any necessary conditions for the reaction to be carried out in the laboratory.

Equation $C_2H_5OH \rightarrow C_2H_4 + H_2O$ (1)

Conditions conc H_2SO_4 or Al_2O_3 } (1) heat or 180° } (1) — (3)

(12)

For examiner's use only

3 When irradiated with ultraviolet light, methane reacts with chlorine to form a mixture containing several organic products.

(a) Name the type of mechanism involved.

free radical (1) — *(1)*

(b) Explain why ultraviolet light is needed.

initiation or break Cl—Cl bond (1)

produce Cl• radicals (1) — *(2)*

(c) Write an equation to show the formation of chloromethane from chlorine and methane.

$CH_4 + Cl_2 \rightarrow CH_3Cl + HCl$ (1) — *(1)*

(d) Another product has a relative molecular mass of 85. Identify this product and write that part of the mechanism which shows its formation from chloromethane.

Product with M_r 85 CH_2Cl_2 (1)

Mechanism $CH_3Cl + Cl\cdot \rightarrow \cdot CH_2Cl + HCl$ (1)

$\cdot CH_2Cl + Cl_2 \rightarrow CH_2Cl_2 + Cl\cdot$ (1) — *(3)*

(e) Explain how a small amount of ethane is formed in the process and name the mechanistic step which leads to its formation.

Explanation two $CH_3\cdot$ radicals join (1)

Name of mechanistic step termination (1) — *(2)*

(f) Give the major product formed when methane reacts with a large excess of chlorine.

CCl_4 or HCl (1) — *(1)*

(10)

Turn over ▶

4 (a) Explain what is meant by the term *nucleophilic substitution*.

replacement (1)

by electron rich species / at electron deficient site (1) (2)

(b) Explain why 1-bromopropane reacts with nucleophiles but propane itself does not.

C—Br polar or δ+ attractive to nucleophiles (1)

C—C, C—H non polar (1) (2)

(c) Write an equation and a mechanism for the reaction of 1-bromopropane with an excess of ammonia.

Equation $CH_3CH_2CH_2Br + NH_3 \longrightarrow CH_3CH_2CH_2NH_2 + HBr$ (1)
($2NH_3$) (NH_4Br)

Mechanism

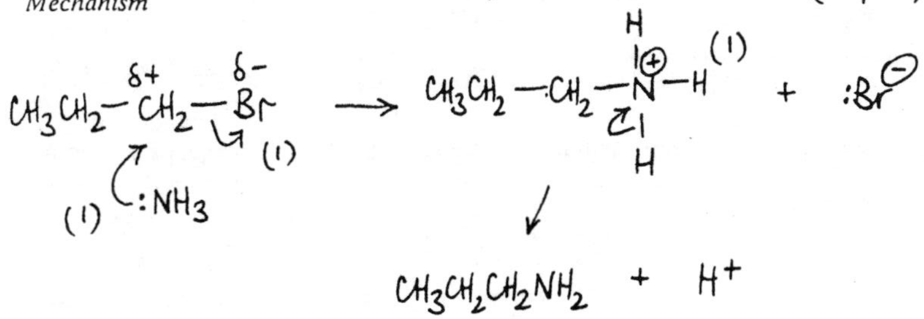

(4)

(d) Give the starting materials and state the conditions for the preparation of CH_3CH_2CN by nucleophilic substitution.

Starting materials CH_3CH_2Br (1) KCN (1)

Conditions aqueous/alcoholic or warm (1) (3)

(11)

5

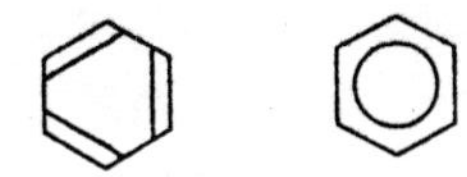

A B

Benzene is sometimes written as structure **A** and sometimes as structure **B**.

(a) What is the significance of the circle in structure **B**?

delocalised electrons (1) (1)

(b) Structure **A** would suggest that benzene would react in the same way as an alkene such as cyclohexene. Give one reaction, other than combustion, that both benzene and cyclohexene will undergo. Write a balanced equation and give any necessary conditions for your example with cyclohexene.

Reaction hydrogenation (1)

Equation for cyclohexene reaction

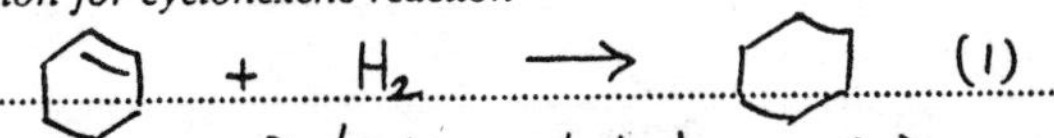

Conditions Pt/Ni catalyst (1) (3)

(c) (i) Choose a reaction that benzene will undergo but cyclohexene will not. For your reaction, write an equation, give the necessary reagents and name the type of mechanism. (NO_2^+) (H^+)

Equation

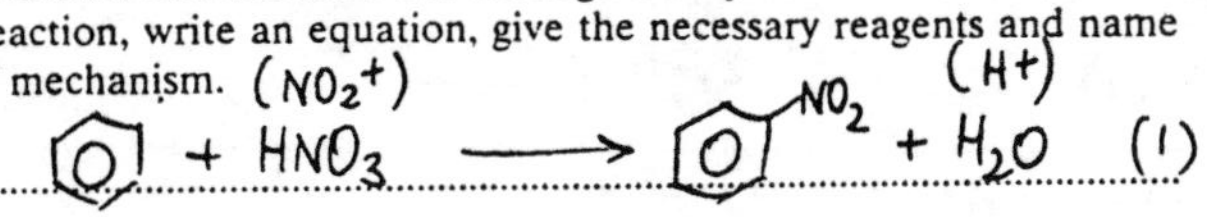

Reagents conc HNO_3 (1) conc H_2SO_4 (1)

Name of mechanism electrophilic substitution (1) (4)

(ii) Choose a reaction that cyclohexene will undergo but benzene will not. For your reaction, write an equation and name and outline the mechanism.

Equation

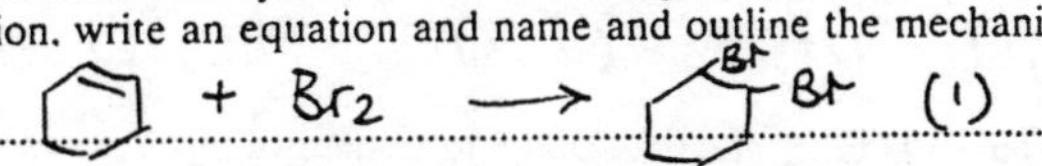

Name of mechanism electrophilic addition (1)

Mechanism

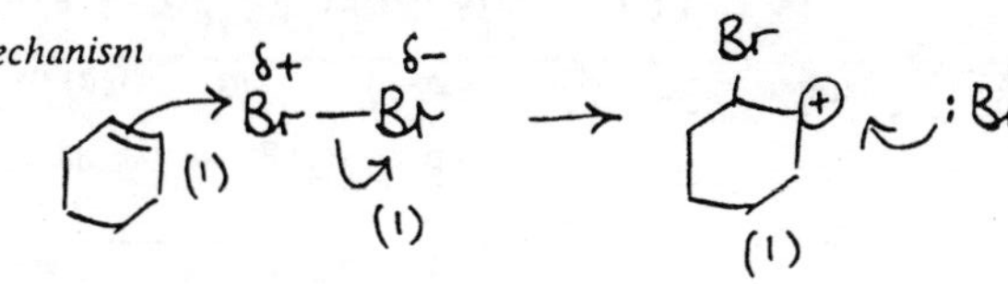

(5)

(13)

CHO3 February 1995 Mark Scheme

Section B Question 6

a)

I	II	III	IV
($CH_3CH_2COOCH_3$)	($CH_3COOCH_2CH_3$)	($HCOOCH_2CH_2CH_3$)	($HCOOCH(CH_3)_2$)
3 peaks (1)	3 peaks (1)	4 peaks (1)	3 peaks (1)
ratio 3 : 2 : 3 (1)	ratio 3 : 2 : 3 (1)	ratio 1 : 2 : 2 : 3 (1)	ratio 1 : 1 : 6 (1)

(Total 8)

b) Given ester has 3 peaks in ratio 3 : 2 : 3

∴ either I or II (1)

Nmr of acid has 3 peaks 3 : 2 : 1 ∴ CH_3CH_2COOH (1)

∴ A must be I ($CH_3CH_2COOCH_3$) (1) (Total 3)

c) Spectrum I has OH but no >C=O (1) ∴ methanol (C) (1)

Spectrum II has >C=O but no OH (1) ∴ ester (A) (1)

Spectrum 3 has >C=O (1) and OH (1) ∴ acid (B) (1)

(max 6)

TOTAL 17

CHO3 February 1995 Mark Scheme

Section B Question 7

a)(i)

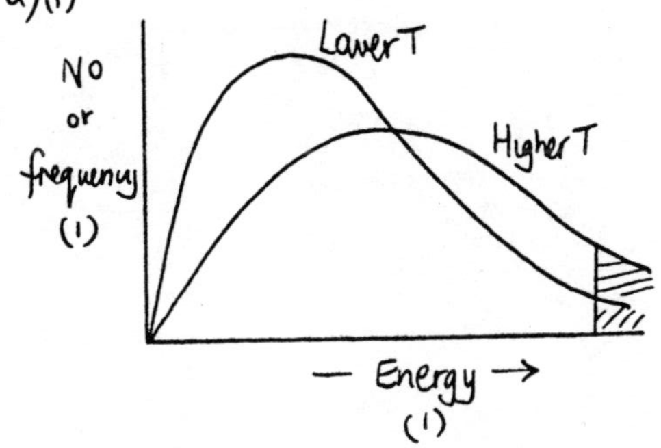

shape of curves (2)

higher T: lower max (1)

displaced to right (1)

(ii) At higher T more molecules (1) have sufficient activation energy (1) to react.

[8]

(b) Rate falls or max rate at start (1)

collisions needed for reaction (1)

At start high concentration/ most reagent molecules (1)

number of molecules falls (1)

fewer collisions (1)

eventually reagents (almost) used up (1)

∴ no collisions between reagent molecules (1)

max [5]

TOTAL 13